KELOWNA

"Partners in Progress" by Mark Zuehlke

Produced in cooperation with the
Kelowna Chamber of Commerce

Windsor Publications, Ltd.
Burlington, Ontario

KELOWNA

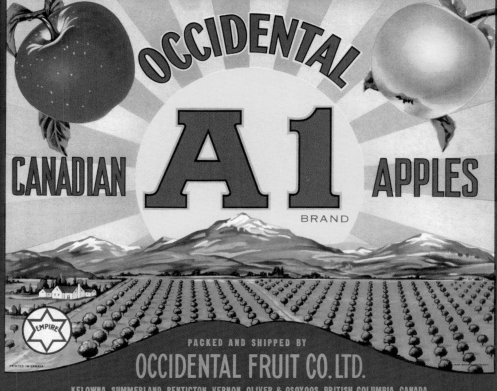

OCCIDENTAL
CANADIAN **A1** BRAND APPLES

PACKED AND SHIPPED BY
OCCIDENTAL FRUIT CO. LTD.
KELOWNA, SUMMERLAND, PENTICTON, VERNON, OLIVER & OSOYOOS, BRITISH COLUMBIA, CANADA

THE ORCHARD CITY

AN ILLUSTRATED HISTORY BY

Ursula Surtees

Windsor Publications, Ltd.—History Books Division

Managing Editor: Karen Story

Design Director: Alexander D'Anca

Staff for *Kelowna: The Orchard City*

Manuscript Editor: Marilyn Horn

Associate Editor: Jeffrey Reeves

Photo Editor: Cameron Cox

Editor, Corporate Biographies: Judith Hunter

Production Editor, Corporate Biographies: Albert Polito

Editorial Assistants: Didier Beauvoir, Thelma Fleischer,
    Kim Kievman, Michael Nugwynne, Kathy B. Peyser,
    Pat Pittman, Theresa Solis

Publisher's Representative: Clarence Jeans

Layout Artist, Corporate Biographies: Michael Burg

Layout Artist: Robaire Ream

Production Assistant: Deena Tucker

Designer: Ellen Ifrah

ISBN: 0-89781-288-3

Windsor Publications, Inc.

Elliot Martin,
Chairman of the Board

James L. Fish, III,
Chief Operating Officer

Michele Sylvestro,
Vice President Sales/Marketing

Frontispiece: Much enjoyed by sportsmen, nevertheless Okanagan Lake is a presence to be respected. Large and very deep, it has its dangerous moods and, some say, its monster—the legendary Ogopogo. Courtesy, Photo/Graphics

Right: Cricket quickly became a Sunday summer-afternoon event. Teams played up and down the valley, all properly attired in white flannels and shirts. The Kelowna Cricket Club is seen here in 1912. Courtesy, Kelowna Museum Association

Contents

"Fruit growing in your Province has acquired the distinction of being a beautiful art as well as a most profitable industry." These words are from a speech given by Canada's governor general Earl Grey to the Royal Agricultural Society in 1905. Photo by Jerg Kroener

Foreword

One year after the City of Kelowna was incorporated, the Board of Trade, later to become the Kelowna Chamber of Commerce, was formed.

From 1906 until the present, members who joined the Association have been active in advertising and promoting the City of Kelowna.

Through the ranks have passed some remarkable men and women who have gone on to make their mark in many fields of endeavor. Notable among these are two premiers of the Province of British Columbia, several mayors of the city, and many other achievers.

True to its original concept, the Kelowna Chamber of Commerce continues to promote and advertise Kelowna, and was instrumental in launching this publication.

Their dedicated service to Kelowna has resulted in many positive actions. The challenges of 1906 were met and overcome, and now as Kelowna stands on the threshold of new discovery via the Coquihalla Highway, the Chamber's role will be intensified.

Kelowna can be confident the tradition will be maintained.

These fur traders
posed after a good sea-
son of trapping some-
time around the turn
of the century. The
snowshoes were a vi-
tal part of their equip-
ment, as the best
pelts were obtained
during the winter.
Courtesy, Kelowna
Museum Association

1

Barren to Beautiful

A vast ice field stretched as far as the eye could see, with here and there a glistening peak upthrust from the cold flat plain. Wind polished the ice as it made its way unhindered over the plateau.

Barely discernible swellings caught frozen granules and fragments as they whipped along the icy surface. Each tiny piece thus caught contributed a minute particle to the slopes.

Occasionally a grinding sound rolled through the air, indicating the mass of ice was shifting and settling more comfortably in the bed it had pressed out for itself.

A thousand years went by, and another thousand. Slowly the swellings—pushed by the pressure of the ice mass—rose inch by slow inch, up and through the snowy crust.

Ridges appeared with eons of accumulated silts in their cracks and crevasses. Soon life in the form of lichens appeared in these scant deposits. Thus began the food chain that was to grow and expand as more time slipped by.

The icy grip of the glacier was relaxing as the climate mellowed. Melting ice

allowed more and more of the ridges to appear, over which passed creatures in search of food: grazers who could feed on the grasses and shrubs, birds whose droppings brought new seed varieties, and predators who ate whatever nature put in their way.

As the ice melted, the water was captured in the early cradles in which the glacier had rested. Around the collected waters the silt deposits, no longer supported by the ice mass, took on an identity of their own. Ringing the depression left by the melting ice, the ridges and silts became ever more dominant. The melted ice became the blue water of a lake some 70 miles long, and the valley to be known as the Okanagan was gradually born.

The hills and waters of the valley hosted many forms of life. Thousands of years later the fossilized evidence of this life would be discovered. The woolly mammoth, giant elk, and a species of bison all made their home in the valley, as well as countless numbers of plants, birds, fish, and insects. The large range of specimens tells of widely diverse climatic conditions.

Okanagan Indians survived for years living off the bounty of the land. Here a group of Okanagans pose under a well-stocked rack of drying fish. Wild deer, roots, and berries were also part of the Indians' diet. Courtesy, Kelowna Museum Archives

Species died out and new ones arrived. In time the mountain slopes were clothed in an assortment of trees, shrubs, and plants which thrived in the shelter of the valley.

The ridges, now grown to mountains, shut off much of the moist flow of weather from the coast. The resulting dry, warm summers and crisp winters provided an almost Eden-like atmosphere in which flourished birds, beasts, fish, and insects of all kinds.

This was the Okanagan Valley as it was when man discovered it. About 7,000 years ago, groups of hunter/gatherer people in search of food came into the valley. Some moved on, some stayed. As they spread throughout the area, territorial boundaries were established. Groups were associated with the territory and sometimes named for the geographic differences in the area of settlement.

The people of this large inland-lake valley became known as the Okanagans. This name over the years has had approximately 46 different spellings. Some of the native people say it means "Big Head," symbolizing the outstanding leadership qualities of the inhabitants. Others believe it possibly refers to the several profile-like mountains in the area. These same profiles were noted by later settlers and given descriptive names such as Giants Head, Black Knight Mountain, and Indian Head—names that are used today.

The Okanagan territory was vast, stretching many miles north and south. These were not agricultural people; they depended on nature to supply their needs. A life-style evolved among the people in harmony with nature's cycles.

Game trails of deer and elk were noted and watched, as were the fish spawning areas. Deer hides were turned into clothing, the bones and antlers into tools, and the meat eaten fresh or dried and stored for winter. Rows and rows of fish, split and flattened, hung in the smoke of fires, or in the wind and sun, drying for winter. The quantity of fish taken at spawning time often meant the difference between survival and starvation in the winter months. Each year the arrival of the spawning fish, chief among them the Kickininee, was awaited with some anxiety. The hope of a heavy run was augmented by appeals to the spirit world, among whom the wily coyote was prominent.

Over the years the Okanagan people discovered the areas that grew edible roots, and the places where wild berries grew in abundance.

Spring signaled the start of movement in the group. Gathering roots as they came into season was the task of the moment and could not be postponed. This was particularly so with plants that were identified by their blooms, including the dainty pink and white blossoms of Sqaakweenum or spring beauty plants, the roots of which are like small round potatoes, and Speetlum or bitterroot. Speetlum roots were gathered in large quantities to be dried and stored for winter use. The pink cactus, like flowers of Speetlum, covered the sloping hillsides and were easily discernible while in bloom, but difficult to locate once that bloom had withered. Saskatoon berries rich in Vitamin C were gathered and dried, as were huckleberries which, when dried, are deliciously sweet and tasty. Wild strawberries and raspberries were mashed into a pulp which could be spread on mats and dried in cake form.

Pottery never evolved among the valley people. Baskets, however, reached a high level of usefulness and beauty. To make these containers it was necessary to gather birch bark and cedar root. The production of cedar-root baskets entailed considerable work. The roots were dug up, then split into strands and woven into tight-coiled baskets so finely constructed they could be used for cooking and storage.

Spear-like bulrush leaves and cylindrical tule reeds were gathered at their peak growth. These were used for making the mats needed for berry drying, and for constructing the quickly assembled summer homes, which could be moved with ease. One simply rolled up the mats, bundled up the support poles, and carried it away. The whole shelter could be transported by one person.

The cold of the interior plateau winters led to the development of an architectural style that, for economy and effectiveness, equals anything that could be designed today using the same material. This was the *kekuli*: the semisubterranean house built by the Okanagans and other Interior Salish tribes.

Constructed over a circular pit, the kekuli formed a four-sided pyramid-like structure made of poles and timbers covered with mats, hides, bark, and earth. A hole in the apex of the pyramid enabled a

The making of a cedar root basket required a considerable amount of time and concentrated effort. Roots were dug up, split into lengthy strands, and tightly woven into baskets to be used for cooking and storage. Photo by T. Hamilton. Courtesy, Kelowna Museum Archives

notched pole to protrude out. The base of the pole was embedded in the floor of the pit, and sloped upward to form a ladder. This was the entrance and exit, which also allowed air in and smoke out. A kekuli could hold quite a number of people; a family could be very comfortable in one.

In these homes, the only permanent ones used, the cold months of winter were passed. This was the time for storytelling, basket making, tool refurbishing, and, sometimes, simply surviving. Situated close to rivers and streams for water, they provided warmth and security during the long cold nights and short days.

With the coming of spring came the renewal of growth and the rounds of visiting the plant areas. The country was full of game—not only deer and elk, but also the black bear and the fearsome grizzly bear.

Kim-ach-touch, the black bear, was plentiful. Its meat was rich and its fur thick. King of the forest was *Kelowna,* the fierce, unpredictable grizzly bear. A hunter taking one of these was brave indeed. The claws and teeth of a grizzly proclaimed the hunter's prowess and could be worn with justifiable pride. Weasels, white in their winter coat, were taken for personal adornment. The pelts contrasted beautifully with the dark hair and eyes of the wearer.

Many legends grew around the birds and beasts of the forests. The coyote was much admired for his cunning and his ability to outwit and out-think his ene-

This subterranean hut, known as a Kekuli, was typical of the shelters inhabited by the Okanagan Indians during the severe winter months. Courtesy, Kelowna Museum Archives

mies. The great owl, gliding silently through the night, kept little children obedient lest they be carried off and hidden away forever.

The Okanagan people learned to use all the natural resources in their territory. They became expert traders with neighbouring tribes and there were gathering places at each end of the lake. Trial and error taught them of the properties of various commodities. Rocks that could be shattered and worked into projectile points or cutting tools were distinguished from those that could be shaped into grinding or pounding tools. Iron oxide in all its shades formed a basic ingredient for the paint used for the pictographs, or rock paintings, found in the Okanagan.

This way of life existed, undisturbed, for many centuries.

The change that came was not occasioned by the mighty grizzly, or by the abundant fish runs, but by an unobtrusive animal that went about its business of cutting trees and building dams. Covered with a highly coveted pelt of strong, gleaming, thick fur, the industrious beaver in his beautiful coat had lured men from the far side of the world, and they were moving inexorably westward.

By the early 1800s tales of these strange people had penetrated into the plateau country. They told of men with pale complexions who had goods and items never seen before. Some of the items found their way into the valley, stimulating much curiosity and a keen interest in acquiring more.

Far to the south, on the mouth of the Columbia River, events were taking place which in a short time would see the end of a life-style that had existed for centuries.

A fur-trading post, Fort Okanogan, was established on the Columbia. The race among the fur companies to corner

new territories was being run with all speed by the traders. In very short order an expedition led by David Stuart of the Pacific Fur Company set out from Fort Okanogan to explore the great valley of which he had heard, laying to the north. The presence of lakes and streams argued well for an abundance of the sought-after beaver. Stuart's men made their way into the great valley in 1811, the first recorded white men to set eyes on the beautiful blue lake and rich green hills.

The central Okanagan was not heavily populated by the native people. It was considered more a hunting and fishing area. Heavier concentrations were at each end of the lake where contacts and trade were easier to establish. The beauty of the valley was perhaps noted but of no particular interest to the fur traders. They concentrated on establishing a trail to the northern interior as far as "Cum-cloups," later to be known as Kamloops, and did indeed establish a trading post there in 1812.

The central Okanagan's only special feature was the large stream which flowed into the lake that was the scene of a heavy fish run in the fall. But to its detri-

The mighty grizzly with his four-inch claws can put fear into anyone crossing his path. The term "grizzly" is used to describe the frosted look on the tips of its hairs. Few in number in the Okanagan, these bears prefer to live in the high country away from settlement. Courtesy, Kelowna Museum Association

ment it was on the opposite side of the lake from the fur trail.

It was not long before the great fur-trading companies realized the folly of continued rivalry, and the two foremost competitors—the Hudson's Bay Company and the North West Company, who had bought out the Pacific Fur Company in 1813—amalgamated. The Fur Brigade Trail was firmly established, and ran almost the entire length of the lake on the west side. Fur brigades, consisting of up to 300 men and horses, passed through bringing goods in and fur bales out.

Fur continued to be the only concern of the people for many years. In 1822 the count of beaver pelts was recorded at 2,251, a worthwhile figure. By 1848 the numbers had dwindled so drastically that only six beavers were brought in. Although changing fashions in Europe decreased the demand for beaver fur, pelts from the otter, mink, marten, ermine, fox, and muskrat were still marketable, so trapping continued.

The impact on the native people was considerable. The whole concept of the hunt had undergone a change. Trapping for trade became of paramount importance. Cloth, guns, shiny copper pots, tea, sugar, and tobacco could be had in exchange for lowly muskrat pelts and other nonfood animals not previously considered worthwhile. A dependency was created, and the traditional life-style eroded, almost to the point of disaster. The deer and other food sources that were not furbearers suitable to the trade were ignored, while the quest for trade

This cairn was erected to commemorate the Old Brigade Trail. This earliest of Okanagan roads was travelled by hundreds of men and horses. It wound its way over mountain passes and along the lake, opening the country to commerce and the outside world. Courtesy, Kelowna Museum Association

pelts was escalated. The inevitable happened. There was a steady decline in furbearers, and much hunger in the winter kekulis when inadequate supplies of meat and fish had been gathered. The time of the cold months became quite desperate on many occasions.

Eventually the Fur Brigade Trail was travelled less and less. When the 49th parallel was established as the border between Canada and the United States in 1846, new trade routes were developed to connect with trails on the Canadian side. The long lines of men and horses were seen no more.

It might have been a considerable time before traffic in any amount came through the valley again, but events, very exciting events, were occurring in the north of British Columbia.

Everywhere in the New World the magical word "gold" had been heard. The Columbia River and California had lured men and women by the thousands to seek their fortunes in the goldfields. So when the news of great finds in the Cariboo in Northern British Columbia leaked out in 1858, the rush to stake claims was on. The Okanagan provided a corridor to the goldfields in the mid-country, and once again the old Fur Brigade Trail was active. Not the long organized lines of previous brigades, but small groups and solitary fortune seekers hurried along it, anxious to pick up the gold they were certain was waiting for them. A few prospectors panned in the Okanagan. Gold was found in several of the creeks, but not in large quantities. With the huge returns being reported from the Cariboo, no one wished to waste their time on such meagre pickings.

There was very little settlement, and most of what existed was geared to trading situations.

When news of gold finds in the Cariboo got out, men and women by the hundreds began to travel via the Okanagan along the old Fur Brigade Trail. Courtesy, Kelowna Museum Archives

In 1861 John McDougal, who had been a packer for the Hudson's Bay Company, was permitted by the company to run a small trading post in which furs and goods could be exchanged. This was located on the east side and approximately mid-way of the lake, close to the large creek where one or two trappers had also settled. This was not an official trading post of the company, but a one-room squared log cabin with one small window, covered with thin scraped rawhide in lieu of glass. In the cabin were stocked such items that had appeal for the native peoples. One of the most favoured trade items was the thick wool HBC blanket. Another favourite was plaid material. The tartans of the Scots, of whom there were many in the fur-trading companies, had caught the eye of many an Indian girl and matron, as did the bright shawls with their long fringes. The Indian men needed ammunition for the guns they had acquired, so lead and powder was carried, and tea, sugar, and tobacco for all.

By the 1860s, it seemed the Okanagan Valley was still to be merely a convenient shortcut to other places and interests. Peo-

These Indian women are seen wearing fringed tartan blankets. Trinkets, tobacco, guns, and fabric were just some of the items introduced by European fur traders in the early 1800s. Courtesy, Kelowna Museum Archives

ple were always hurrying along to other dreams. In all those hundreds of square miles, only a few scattered log cabins existed, inhabited by fur trappers who had no wish to see permanent settlement taking over their trap-line country.

The turn of the century was a time of renewed growth for the city of Kelowna. Lawson's General Store was situated on Bernard Avenue in the early 1900s. It carried a full range of dry goods, lamps, kitchen utensils, and housewares of all kinds. Courtesy, Kelowna Museum Association

2

They Came to a Valley

The Far West had many challenges. While many came to the West looking for riches or freedom, others were moved by different concerns. The churchmen of Britain and Europe saw an opportunity, and felt an enormous responsibility, to gather up a spiritual harvest on the frontier.

Fast on the heels of the fur traders came the missionaries. Often armed with little more than their faith, they faced incredible hardships and privations. Some gave their lives for their faith; others suffered severe health problems, starvation, and —most cruel of all to them—indifference to their solicitations. Whether in the light of history the missionaries are to be judged right or wrong, no one can deny their faith in their vision, and the zeal with which it was pursued.

In the Northwest it was primarily the Oblates that moved into the newly opened areas. To these men we are indebted for a contemporary look at the new country and new people they encountered. Long and detailed letters were sent to their superiors, full of hopes, fears, anguish, and pleas. Customs of the people, terrain, climate, and wild-

life were all reported on, as were the soil's potential for providing sustenance (missionaries often depended on the mercy of the land for food) and the number of people (Indian and non-Indian) in the area.

Requests for supplies were constant, and often sporadically responded to. The joy that even the smallest items brought is clearly illustrated in a letter written in 1857 by one of those isolated Western Oblates.

Brother Joseph was beside himself with gladness when his eyes fell on the little packages of seeds, the files, scissors, and other similar objects. Accept, in fine, our thanks for the piece of broadcloth you sent us; by this favor we continue to be "Black Gowns."

Ah! With my whole heart I wish that you could have seen us as we were opening the boxes. Each object excited new cries of joy and augmented our grateful love for the donors. All arrived in good order. The snuff had got a little mixed with the clover-seed, but no matter! My nose is not very delicate. It is the first donation

The tall figure and booming voice of Father Pandosy became familiar to Indians and whites alike. Hardworking and dedicated, it is said that he took great pleasure in teaching the Indian people music and singing. Courtesy, Kelowna Museum Association

The tall figure and booming voice of Father Pandosy became familiar to Indians and whites alike. Hardworking and dedicated, it is said that he took great pleasure in teaching the Indian people music and singing. Courtesy, Kelowna Museum Association

sent into these mountains, at least since I have been here.

In spite of the hardships the missionaries continued their work, and small groups of Oblates continued to make their way into the West. By 1838 these new Catholic missions had an urgent need for more workers. The response to this request was long in coming, but in 1847 more Oblate workers did at last make their way into the land of the Yakima and Cayuse Indians, in what is now the state of Washington. The territory to which they came was far from serene; a nearby Protestant missionary/doctor, Dr. Marcus Whitman, and his wife had been murdered by the Cayuse.

Among the new Oblates was 23-year-old Charles Felix Adolph Pandosy. Young Charles had given up the comfortable life he enjoyed as son of a landowning family near Marseilles to become an Oblate. His family position had given him an education, and nature had bestowed upon him an imposing physique, good humour, and a strong voice—a voice that would reach out in song and prayer to the converts he was seeking to make.

The tense situation at the Yakima River required an immediate need for firm leadership. Bishop Norbert Blanchet decided on what amounted to a "field promotion." He ordained Pandosy and passed him quickly through the hierarchy in only eight days.

Father Pandosy was given the task of establishing a mission. The "black robes" were looked upon with suspicion, but in spite of this Father Pandosy managed to gain the friendship of the chief of the Yakimas.

But there was still much hostility. During an Indian uprising that took the lives of the Whitmans, the Oblates were in the unhappy position of being suspected by both the whites and the Indians. The whites suspected Father Pandosy of aiding his Indian flock, while the Indians weren't entirely convinced that he was not assisting the whites. News of happenings in the territories was scant. In 1856 a report trickled out that Father Pandosy had been killed. Although this proved untrue, the Oblates were obviously in a very precarious situation.

Thus it was that the Oblates arranged for their removal to the hinterland of New Caledonia, which later became the province of British Columbia. Father Pandosy made plans for the group to separate: one group would procure horses, the other would gather supplies. The groups finally reunited and together made their way north into Canadian territory.

Here too their presence was regarded by the natives with suspicion.

Fortunately one of the guides, Cyprian Lawrence, had married Therese, an Indian girl of the Flat Head tribe. She was related to a chief of the Okanagans. Grudgingly the chief gave the missionaries permission to go unmolested into the Okanagan Valley. His niece Therese had pointed out that if anything happened to the white men, one of whom was her husband, the chief would have to provide for her as was required of a kinsman.

The little group made its way into the heart of the Okanagan Valley. Father Pandosy wrote his superiors in October of 1859 that they had settled on a campsite on a small lake, later to be known as Duck Lake. This lay parallel to the great Okanagan Lake.

Winter was fast approaching and the missionaries were ill-prepared. They spent a wretched and hungry winter at Duck Lake. The shallow water froze readily around the edges so even procuring a good water supply was difficult. They were forced to eat the horses, which probably would have perished anyway from lack of feed.

After such a hard winter it was obvious to the Oblates that a new settlement area had to be sought. They finally decided on a permanent settlement 12 miles south of their original choice.

This was a far superior spot. Acres of flatland surrounded them and a full flowing river was close by. It was the fall of 1860.

The skeptical Indians were still suspicious of the white men. Why would these

The Pandosy Mission site is an oasis of peace and tranquility. The two buildings in the centre are the original chapel and sleeping quarters. On the right is a double log-wall construction storage house. This scenic area with its trees and grassy surroundings remains today within the boundaries of the City of Kelowna. Courtesy, Kelowna Museum Association

men in their long black gowns want to live among them? What was their motive? The Indian's hostility grew.

Father Pandosy had, by this time, over a decade of experience with the Indian people. He must have had a remarkable understanding of their temperament. It was at this most difficult time, the story goes, that Father Pandosy felt that actions could best demonstrate his determination to stay. At the next show of hostility the good father calmly walked over to a large tree. He took his knife from its sheath at his waist, and with the sharp tip traced the outline of a man upon the standing trunk. Then, stepping back, he took what appeared to be casual aim and threw it at the outline. The knife flew with a satisfying "thunk" into the heart of the figure. Silently Father Pandosy walked over, pulled out the knife, and re-sheathed it. The hostile Indians melted away, and from that time on regarded this large white man with new respect. Soon his booming voice became well-known and he became a good friend to the Indians, loved and respected throughout the valley.

The name given the new settlement was L'Anse au Sable, or Sandy Creek. It was not long before the first little squared log building was in place and the first seeds in the ground, the very first agricultural settlement in the interior of British Columbia. Little did Father Pandosy dream that this same small building would survive to become a Provincial Historical Site some 125 years later, and part of a city named Kelowna.

The name of L'Anse au Sable had short use. The river became more popularly known as Mission River or Mission Creek, a name it retains to this day.

The missionaries encouraged other settlers to come and take up land. They suc-cessfully attracted a number of enterprising people, among them Eli and Marie Louise Lequime. Eli and his family had been among the gold seekers at Rock Creek some miles distant. They came to the mission settlement and perceived that a store and stopping place would be needed for the increasing number of travellers finding their way into the interior.

Mrs. Lequime is reported to have been an excellent businesswoman. She was also the first recorded white woman in the area. Marie Louise was made of stern stuff and filled the role of dentist, using a primitive but effective instrument known as a tooth puller.

Father Pandosy's flock increased and settlement grew with the mission as its centre. In due course a shining white church complete with a steeple was erected. A bell was ordered from France to hang in the steeple.

The story of the church bell and Rosa Casorso can be called "stranger than fiction." Giovanni Casorso had worked as a packer and first met Father Pandosy in 1883. Like many others, Giovanni had left behind a wife and family in Italy. As Giovanni made his way in the New World and secured land, his one desire was to be reunited with his family. So his wife Rosa and their three young children set sail for Canada.

After arriving in San Francisco, Rosa had absolutely no means of finding her way into the hinterland of British Columbia. Tired out from her long sea voyage, and with a very small vocabulary of English, Rosa was at her most distraught. Then came the miracle. On the docks in San Francisco was a large crate, marked with the name of its destination: Okanagan Mission. Inside the crate was the church bell. Rosa's only link to her new homeland was a paper on which was writ-

ten "Okanagan Mission." The bell became her lifeline, and she followed it from that moment on. Where the bell stopped, Rosa stopped; when it continued its journey, so did Rosa. The bell and Rosa finally arrived safely at Okanagan Mission on a stagecoach.

Rosa's first home in the settlement was very humble—just a little, low log house with a sod-covered roof—but it belonged to her and her family, on their own land. In time another house was built, which grew as the family grew. As the Casorso family was a large one, the house eventually was of a substantial and rather imposing size. It still stands today in unspoiled green surroundings.

The Casorsos were hard workers. They established a market garden that produced vegetables for local trade and nearby towns, especially the mining communities which had little time to farm. The Casorso children showed the same hardworking streak as their parents. Between them, they established a large cattle- and meat-marketing business, which ran hundreds of head of cattle, and operated the Sanitary Meat Market in later years. Casorso onions and Casorso pigs became famous throughout the province.

The hardworking and determined Casorso family added to their farmland and stock until they became one of the biggest suppliers of meat and vegetables in the area. The family is still well-represented in the Okanagan today. Courtesy, Kelowna Museum Association

In Canada Lord Aberdeen was honoured by the Blackfoot and Six Nation Indians with two names, "Clear-Sky" and "Sitting Down White Buffalo Calf." He was given brightly embroidered and beaded buckskins to wear as an honorary tribal member. Courtesy, Kelowna Museum Association

Like the Casorsos, the Catholic Church was very industrious in early Kelowna, serving the area alone for 30 years. During that time Father Pandosy had been moved around the province, but had returned in his later years to the Okanagan Mission settlement. In 1891 he died as he had lived, serving the people.

Responding to a call from Keremeos, Father Pandosy, although ailing himself, went on his long cold ride of duty. His condition worsened. Fatigue and cold caught up with him on his return trip and by the time he reached Penticton he was very ill indeed. Chief Francois of the Penticton band took him to his cabin, but in spite of all that could be done, Father Pandosy could not rally. He died in the arms of his old Indian friend. With sorrow, his body was brought back to the mission to be buried and, sad to say, forgotten, until recent efforts to locate the old graveyard were successful. Now his resting place is marked with a plaque set in a boulder, a few hundred yards from his still-standing mission buildings.

During his lifetime Father Pandosy had attempted to promote schooling among the Indians and settlers. It was a short-lived effort, although a travelling cleric commented on the quality of singing achieved at the mission school.

The native children found it hard to follow a set school regime and the non-Indian children were needed at home as soon as they were big enough to work.

It wasn't until 1873 that a schoolhouse was built. The government purchased William Smithson's house for a school. That, as it turned out, was the easy part. Securing a teacher took a while longer. It was not until December of 1875 that one was found in the person of Angus McKenzie. His salary was $60 per month. He was also supplied, free of charge, meat, butter, milk, eggs, and firewood.

McKenzie taught until 1878 and brought his 21 pupils along admirably. The superintendent reported in 1877:

Children who eighteen months before were utterly ignorant of the simplest rudiments, and unable to speak a word of English had advanced so rapidly as to be able, when the school was visited, to read clearly and fluently in the fourth reader.

Many more changes would come to the Okanagan in the 1890s as a result of a visit by a prominent Scottish nobleman. The Earl of Aberdeen and his wife, the Lady Isabel, travelled through the Okana-

Facing page: August Gillard pre-empted land on the shores of Okanagan Lake when there were very few settlers or permanent buildings. He adapted the Indian winterhouse style to his own needs, and was one of the first people to build on what is now the site of the City of Kelowna. Courtesy, Kelowna Museum Association

Below: The SS *Aberdeen* makes a winter trip on the Okanagan. A messenger in the truest sense, she brought news from up and down the valley. She made her appointed runs year round and was a focal point of life in the Okanagan. Courtesy, Kelowna Museum Association

gan in 1891 and fell in love with the valley. Perhaps it was the mountains and lakes—so like those in the Highlands—that beguiled them. Whatever the cause, their love of the area was to shape the history of the valley.

By the late 1800s there were some 400 settlers in the area, many of them from an English/Scottish background. These settlers had been brought up with the Anglican and Presbyterian disciplines and felt a need for a place of worship. It was of some concern to Lady Aberdeen that there was no Presbyterian church for her countrymen to attend, so she started the move to achieve one. In 1892 the Benvoulin Presbyterian Church was raised, its pews arranged in typical curved Presbyterian fashion. The small, beautifully proportioned church served the Presbyterians for many years and was supported by mission funds.

The Aberdeens had envisaged a townsite near the mission. Settlement had up

to that time been in and around that general area. They themselves had bought a large acreage and called it Guisachan, Gaelic for "Place of the Firs," after Lady Aberdeen's childhood home. The presence of such a prestigious landowner, later to become Canada's governor general, brought in many new settlers. So much so that the Canadian Pacific Railway suddenly realized that the area was a potential investment opportunity. Train service did not extend through the valley so a link of transport, a stern-wheeler, was put on Okanagan Lake. It was named the SS *Aberdeen*.

Astute businesspeople realized that the stern-wheeler would bring more people in and a good wharf would be needed. The mission was situated away from the lakeshore, so in 1892 a new townsite was laid out on the lake's edge.

As the settlers debated over a name for the new townsite, an amusing incident was recalled concerning August Gil-

lard, who had pre-empted land nearby 30 years before. It seems that Gillard, seeing the serviceable winter kekulis of the Indians, built one for himself. One day a group of passing Indians, seeing the smoke rising from the kekuli, called to see who was there. Out came Gillard, with a fur cap pulled over his abundant hair, and his face covered with a good crop of whiskers. The Indians were delighted and, clapping their hands, cried "Kim-a-touch! Kim-a-touch!" —meaning "black bear," or "bear face."

So the settlers considered Kim-a-touch as a name. But it had a very guttural pronunciation, and the more melodious Kelowna, or grizzly bear, was chosen instead.

The new town consisted of five buildings set in a row on the south side of the main street. For several years no building took place on the north side as it bordered on land owned by rancher A.B. Knox. He ran cattle on the land and the

The first service in the new town was held in Lequime's upstairs room in 1894. The following year the little Anglican church of St. Michael and All Angels was built. Like the others it was of wood construction.

The Reverend Thomas E. Greene at first travelled to Kelowna once a month to hold services. In 1897 he moved to Kelowna to become the first permanent Anglican minister. The Reverend Greene, later to become archdeacon, was a man of great integrity and humility with a gentle nature that made him much loved. A true father to his congregation, he became "Daddy" Greene to one and all. He performed the marrying, christening, and burial services for 30 years in his religious role. So upright and honest was the Reverend that he developed another role of trust. It was not uncommon for miners in the nearby mining towns, where the Reverend Greene also preached, to give him their hard-won gold and earnings. This he transported to the designated place of deposit. One miner, who had used the Reverend's goodwill delivery service for some years, gave "Daddy" Greene enough gold to have a ring made for himself. There was enough for a heavy, wide gold band. When the Reverend Greene died, the ring was cut into three narrower bands, one for each of his daughters.

A new dressed-stone church was begun in 1911 and completed in 1913. This later St. Michaels and All Angels Church, complete with beautiful stained-glass windows, is still the main Anglican church in Kelowna today. Preparations are in place to dedicate it as a cathedral, thus making Kelowna one of our few Western cathedral cities.

The Methodists built their first church in the new town in 1903-1904 and the Baptists laid the cornerstone of their church

Bernard Lequime, like his father, Eli, was an astute businessman. He helped lay out the new townsite of Kelowna and was among the first to build there. Kelowna's main downtown street, Bernard Avenue, is named for him. Courtesy, Kelowna Museum Association

first sound heard by many travellers coming into Kelowna on the SS *Aberdeen* was the bawling of cattle.

From then on building and settlement concentrated on this new location. Bernard Lequime, son of Eli, helped to lay out the townsite and the main street was named Bernard in his honour. He was one of the first to build on the new site, and his building had a meeting room upstairs.

The Anglicans, still with no permanent church, held meetings in various places whenever a minister was available.

George Rose was a talented writer with a flair for capturing the essence of the issues in his editorials. Nothing escaped comment, and he was a constant spur to the citizens of Kelowna during his years as owner and editor of the *Kelowna Courier*. Courtesy, Kelowna Museum Association

in 1907. The Catholic Church, finding the congregation moving away from the mission site, built a new church in Kelowna in 1911. When it was completed, the bell Rosa Casorso had followed so faithfully was moved again and hung in the new bell tower, where its clear voice continued to call in the worshipers.

In less than a decade Kelowna citizens, some 1,800 in number, had raised five new churches. Seventy-six years later, in 1987, there were 31 different faiths represented in Kelowna, including Buddhism, Mormonism, and Interdenominationalism.

Church development was not the only activity in Kelowna's early years. Much was happening in the area as the heart of settlement in the central Okana-

gan moved from the mission to Kelowna by the lake.

Among the many well-educated settlers drawn to the valley were the Rose brothers, George and Hugh. Of Scottish background, and with a strong sense of duty and responsibility, the brothers first tried their hand at fruit ranching. George, however, had other talents, and he sought an outlet for them.

In July 1904 R.H. Speddings established Kelowna's first newspaper, the *Kelowna Clarion*. In October 1905 George Rose took it over. He had finally found his niche. Editorials poured forth from Rose's pen. Two items were constantly commented on: the need for an efficient fire brigade and equipment; and, of even greater importance, the incorporation of Kelowna

Facing page, top: Polo playing required good horses and lots of stamina. It was exciting both to play and to watch. A number of good fields were kept up to provide suitable playing grounds. One of the most popular was at the foot of Knox Mountain. Courtesy, Kelowna Museum Association

Facing page, bottom: Lawn parties, afternoon tea, and croquet were all considered an essential part of Kelowna's social life. Everyone came to these events either as participants or as spectators. Long white "lawn" dresses were considered proper attire for young ladies, and gentlemen wore jackets even on the warmest of days. Courtesy, Kelowna Museum Association

into a city. Sound principles of government were essential, along with a tax base to implement them. Incorporation must come. Spurred by Rose's passionate editorials, a petition was presented to the lieutenant-governor, with 229 signatures of qualified voters.

On May 4, 1905, Kelowna received its articles of incorporation. The charter provided for a mayor and five aldermen. George Rose had not been alone in his ideas. A number of businessmen were in agreement. When the task of electing a mayor and council was set about, these businessmen were on hand to form the first council.

Henry Raymer, an architect and a builder who had come to the Okanagan in 1892, was elected mayor. Kelowna has many fine buildings designed and built by this first mayor. Included in these was the Raymer Block which, besides being a major business establishment, was the social hub of the city. Upstairs was a dance hall and an opera house.

The aldermen covered a great range of talent. Included were Daniel Wilbur Sutherland, known to everyone as D.W. He was the first schoolteacher in the Kelowna townsite, arriving to teach in the cold February of 1893. It was so cold that the lake froze that year. His class was held in Lequime's well-used upstairs room, after he and one of his scholars coaxed some warmth out of the stove so that hats and mitts could be removed.

David Lloyd-Jones was a real old-timer, having come into the valley in 1880. Later he was to take over the sawmill started by Lequime and built it (in spite of several fires) into an expanded and a thriving business.

Elisha Baily, an astute negotiator, was active in establishing co-operative marketing with the Kelowna Shippers Union.

Simon Elliott, known to all as Sam, started out in the blacksmith business. He was a large man and looked every inch the part of blacksmith. As time went on Elliott made the switch from horses to the horseless carriage, and managed the first motorcar dealership in town where he sold McLaughlin and Tudhope-McIntyre cars. The latter was a chain-driven vehicle, one of which still exists in Kelowna today as a part of the Kelowna Museum Collections. Each year it chugs its way the length of Bernard Avenue in the annual Kelowna Regatta Parade.

Colin Smith was of "gentlemen" stock. Son of a governor of British Guiana, Smith had great curiosity and character. He explored the potential of tobacco growing in the area, and put a great deal of his own money into it. In 1903 he formed the Kelowna Club and endeavoured to form a board of trade that same year. He liked to ride fine buckskin-coloured horses, and was dubbed "Buckskin Smith" by close friends and associates.

This then was the mayor and council who took on the job of running the city in 1905. The tax assessment for running Kelowna was $3,537.10 for 1906.

George Rose was not on that first council. Perhaps he felt his freedom as an editor would be handicapped. He had, however, been made a justice of the peace at the ripe age of 25. He remained editor of the *Clarion* (renamed the *Kelowna Courier* in 1905) for many years. The *Kelowna Courier* is still published daily as part of the Thompson newspaper chain.

Kelowna attracted many young men and women of good family and educated background at the turn of the century. The city experienced an influx of settlers with considerably more than just their two hands as a means to achieve a living. Many of these English/Scottish settlers

came from wealthy backgrounds. Not for them the log shack and making-do. Fine homes were built, and music, poetry readings, theatre, cricket matches, and afternoon teas were considered essential to a "proper" life-style. Ladies rode sidesaddle, and elegant white afternoon dresses were worn to lawn parties. Young men quickly established polo and sailing clubs, laid out flower gardens, and held paper chases in lieu of fox hunting.

There were also, of course, young families with children. The school near the mission was still going strong, but now a school was a necessity for the growing town population.

D.W. Sutherland had an enrollment of 28 in that first school over Lequime's store. But that meeting room was soon outgrown, and a small one-room school was built in 1894. This could accommodate 35 pupils. The work, contracted by H.W. Ray-

The Boy Scout movement was sound training for many young Kelowna men. Most of the boys pictured here made their mark as leaders of the community. Camping, sports, and general organizing skills were taught, as well as team cooperation. Courtesy, Kelowna Museum Association

mer, was to include everything from the blackboards to the outside latrine.

Although a great improvement, the school was soon hopelessly outgrown. In 1904, a wood-structured, white-painted schoolhouse was built and served well. But it too overflowed and soon another building was needed.

By 1908 the school trustees asked the city to purchase two lots as a new school site. This was put to a vote but was defeated, although the vote to *build* a new school was passed by a single vote. It would take two more rounds at the polls before the trustees won their case and the purchase was approved soundly by 103 votes for, 47 against.

The brochure for 1912-1913 comments on the fact that Kelowna now had three schools. The latest new "public" school was pronounced "excellent." Excellent it may have been, but for sheer unattractiveness this new seat of learning would be hard to beat. The name "Bleak House" springs to mind when viewing this gaunt, tall, brick building that took itself very seriously.

Even as the 1913 brochure was going to print, plans were in place to build yet another school. This one, as if in reaction to the downright ugliness of the previous one, was a dream school, brick built and of pleasing proportions. Set on sweeping lawns, this school had an imposing en-

trance of broad steps and stately pillars. It was officially opened in grand style January 20, 1914. Both of these schools are still standing. The "ugly sister" of the two has been enlarged and facelifted and serves now as the new headquarters for the Boys and Girls Club. The pillared beauty is untouched—older, but still elegant on its green lawn. Almost across from it stands Kelowna Senior Secondary School, completed in 1939. It too was a brick beauty but suffered severe damage in a fire in December 1979. It was rebuilt and is the largest school of the Kelowna district.

There were some families that felt education in the "colonies" fell short of the standards they themselves had experienced.

So a private school for the children of gentlemen was established. This school, Chesterfield Hall, taught the arts and classics. At the same time Mackies School was established at the north end of the valley. This school was run on the lines of an English boarding school for boys. Mackies School won the "Battle for the Boys." Young gentlemen from all over British Columbia went to this school. Chesterfield Hall closed its doors, but Mackies ran well into the 1930s.

Kelowna's growth continued and the school district expanded. Numbered School District 23, it encompasses today a very large area extending well beyond the city of Kelowna boundaries, to in-

The Benvoulin School is seen here in 1912. This school was the second on the site, the first, established in 1874, having been outgrown. In time it, too, was supplanted by a third school, which later gave way to the main administration office of School District #23. The children are seen here setting off on a parade. Courtesy, Kelowna Museum Association

clude a number of regional districts. In it there are now 34 elementary schools and nine junior/senior high schools. The headquarters of School District 23 is situated on the very same site as the school built close to the old mission site in 1874. Kelowna is also the main site of Okanagan College and Vocational School, which has campuses throughout the valley. Kelowna also has French Immersion classes for parents who wish their children to be bilingual, and several schools run independently by religious orders.

Kelowna schools have produced scholars and sportsmen in many fields. A fine group effort was the Kelowna Senior Secondary Boys Rugby Team which went to Britain to play the top Rugby teams of Welsh and English schools in 1980.

During Kelowna's early years, as the children were taught in new schools, the adults were kept well-informed by the indefatigable George Rose, whose editorials and comments ran unchallenged in the *Kelowna Courier*—the only newspaper in the city for several years. When C.H. Leathley proposed that a second newspaper be established, the city council did not receive the suggestion with enthusiasm. Undaunted, Leathley decided he would publish anyway. The first issue of the *Orchard City Record* was out in December of 1908. Two years later, the paper was taken over by Leathley's brother, John.

Much later, in July of 1930, the *Kelowna Capital News* began offering a small weekly advertising service, sprinkled throughout with little tidbits of news and comments from the editor. The *Capital News* maintained this neighbourly format for many years. During World War II the editor wrote a personal letter to every man and woman from Kelowna serving overseas. Many replied from such places as England, Scotland, Italy, France, and Belgium. The editor, Les Kerry, kept all of

these letters, which subsequently became a wonderful collection of first-hand wartime experiences.

The *Orchard City Record* ceased publication in 1920. The *Capital News* now publishes twice weekly. Its news base has expanded, but it still runs a complete advertising service.

In 1931 Kelowna reached out to an even wider audience. It was in that year that the first radio station, "The Voice of the Okanagan," hit the airwaves. This station started from small beginnings.

In 1912 George Dunn operated an amateur radio transmitter; then, in the early 1920s he operated on phone frequencies with the licenced call letters 10-AY. It was James William Bromley-Browne who saw the potential and future of radio. In 1931 he took over 10-AY and lifted it out of the amateur status and on to the airwaves as CKOV.

Early days of Kelowna broadcasting used a great deal of local talent. Well-played musical instruments and good singing voices could be found in Kelowna. Bromley-Browne had a resonant voice that was heard throughout the valley during the 1930s and 1940s.

It happens that occasionally technology comes into conflict. During these early broadcasting days, William John Knox, an early doctor in Kelowna, became intrigued with the possible benefits of electrical impulse equipment in the practice of medicine. Dr. Knox had in his office a number of electrical chargers for various medical treatments. It was soon observed that broadcasting seemed to become somewhat erratic during the doctor's treatment times. With this discovery a schedule was made so that both broadcasting and medicine would be satisfied, and coordinated technology was practiced from then on.

In the 1950s, when the Kelowna Packers (the home-town hockey team) played, everyone gathered around the radio for the play-by-play commentary that was regularly broadcast. Kelownans took their hockey seriously; woe betide those who interrupted these sessions with idle chatter.

Over the years CKOV has kept its family flavour. New Year's Eve was always special. On what must have been one of British Columbia's earliest "phone-ins," people from up and down the valley would phone the station and, over the air, wish the Brownes and all their friends and neighbours a "Happy New Year." This practice was continued well into the 1950s.

The next generation of Brownes was also a James, better known as "Big Jim" Browne. Following in his father's footsteps, Big Jim watched over and guided the station through the 1950s and 1960s. By this time it employed up to 20 people.

The third generation is yet another James, and an independent one. Jamie Browne was determined to learn the business thoroughly. Not satisfied with the easy step of inherited management as the boss' son, Jamie quit the station. He came back when he felt he was able to do a competent job on his own merits. In 1987 he was awarded British Columbia's highest honour as Broadcaster of the Year.

CKOV has been in business 63 years on AM and several years ago introduced Kelowna's first FM station, FM104. Together these two stations employ 35 people and offer programmes of international and local interests. In November 1987 CKOV won the Canadian Association of Broadcasters top community-service award. In 1988 CKOV changed ownership, but is still very community oriented.

In 1971 Kelowna's second AM radio station, CKIQ, came into being. Established by Bob Hall and Walter Gray, who already had a following from the radio station in Salmon Arm, located some 60 miles north of Kelowna, they introduced programming with a Western touch. Throughout the years this has been expanded to

The Okanagan's very own C.H.B.C serves 55 communities within its covered area. In this photo, feature producer Mike Roberts interviews a construction foreman on the progress of a controversial highway. Courtesy, C.H.B.C.-T.V.

a broader spectrum, particularly in sports. CKIQ's transmitter tower is situated within a few hundred yards of Father Pandosy's little log mission buildings.

Kelowna's second FM station came about as a result of the persistence of Nick Frost. It was Frost's thought that Kelowna was ready to support another FM station. He tried unsuccessfully for several years to get the necessary licencing to establish one. Persistence paid off, and in 1985 SILK FM was born. Its very apt slogan is "Beautiful Music for a Beautiful City."

Reading and listening were to be Kelowna's informational exchange until 1957. This was the year television made its debut. The people of Kelowna joined the world in loving Lucy on "I Love Lucy." "Father Knows Best" and "Life of Riley" were discussed in Kelowna kitchens and cof-

fee shops, and Sergeant Friday entranced everyone while getting "just the facts ma'am" on "Dragnet." With television a whole new vista was opened up to the Okanagan Valley.

Television was the realization of a dream of the owners of the three major radio stations of the valley: CKOK Penticton in the south, CKOV Kelowna in the central Okanagan, and CJIB Vernon at the north end of the valley. This was truly a collaborative effort. The feasibility of three separate stations for each of the communities was examined, and the decision to combine into one central station was made. This was to be in Kelowna, at a cost of more than a quarter-million dollars. The master transmitter is situated at the summit of Blue Grouse Mountain, an elevation of 4,500 feet. With expansion and technical advances, CHBC-TV now has 27 relay transmitters carrying programmes to 55 communities.

The early studio with its staff of 12 was in an upgraded garage. It still is, only now it has a new facade and a honeycomb of offices and studios, all of which are kept busy serving the approximately 240,000 viewers. This requires a staff of 56 and a fleet of mobile production units.

CHBC-TV gives coverage on all subjects. Although it has grown, it still maintains good community involvement. Its current programme manager Terry Mahoney is making sure that the Okanagan people can retain their feeling of being part of their TV station with programmes reflecting local input and interests.

The Okanagan Valley spent its early years in geographic isolation. To get to Kelowna one always had to pass through a mountain range. On the one side are the Rockies and the Monashees, and on the other the Cascades and Coast ranges. In the winter months this isolation was aggravated by heavy snowfalls closing roads through the mountain passes.

Those early newspapers, radio stations, and, later, television stations put the valley in daily contact not only with each other, but the rest of the world.

Sophisticated communications systems of today have eliminated the informational isolation of former years, and the advent of television has allowed Kelowna to be "on the spot" with all important events. That this should come about without sacrificing the community flavour reflects the roots of Kelowna's media, all of which have been "home grown."

There were many talented musicians in Kelowna. Small concert groups provided music on occasions that required sounds more mellow than that provided by the brass and percussion of the city band. This was especially so on early radio broadcasts. Courtesy, Kelowna Museum Associaiton

This fruit display more than justified Kelowna's title of "The Orchard City." Varieties of apples in shades varying from pale green to rosy red were displayed. Note the size of the apples displayed on the floor in the foreground. Courtesy, Kelowna Museum Association

3

The Orchard City

The earliest reports of the Okanagan had all emphasized the potential for cattle raising in the area. This, combined with mining activities in other parts of the province, influenced the land use. Cattle were raised and sent off to provide meat to the miners. The cattle and the attendant need for hay crops required large acreages. Rangeland was quickly taken up, and as the number and size of herds increased, the ranchers added to their holdings. This situation curtailed the development of the valley, as it could only sustain a limited number of these huge ranches.

This was the situation when the Earl and Countess of Aberdeen visited. They sized up the situation with great perception and personal optimism. They were convinced that the only way to open up this beautiful valley to its full potential was to encourage more settlement.

But what enticed people to *this* valley over all others? Its assets were its climate, the lake, and its altitude, all of which combined to make a healthy environment for family life. Its major drawback

was the shortage of available land. Land there was, in plenty, but most of the best belonged to, or was leased by, the cattle ranchers.

The Aberdeens had held many responsible government positions. Ireland in particular had reason to bless them. During the time that Lord Aberdeen was lord-lieutenant of Ireland, both he and Lady Aberdeen worked to improve conditions for the poor. Lady Aberdeen had, through tremendous personal effort, created the "Irish Village" at the Chicago World's Fair to promote interest and sales of the Irish lace cottage industry, thus putting at least a meagre income into countless otherwise penniless homes. Later they returned to Ireland to wage a war on tuberculosis, which was occurring in epidemic proportions at the time.

Their commitment and energy was now put to work to develop the Okanagan. This attitude, linked with the observation of produce harvested, led to their decision to purchase a ranch of 480 acres on the shores of Okanagan Lake. This was to be turned into orchards. Writing

of the Okanagan in 1891, Lady Aberdeen stated:

Up to now but little attention has been devoted to fruit growing, as this has been principally a stock raising country, but the possibilities shown by the few orchards already planted, point to its being found to possess exceptional advantages for the pursuit of this industry.

Lady Aberdeen's brother, Coutts Marjoribanks (pronounced "Marshbanks"), was to manage the ranch while they returned to Scotland. A return visit to Canada was planned, as was further investment. When a very large block of land in the north end of the valley became available for purchase, the Aberdeens bought it, all 13,000 acres. This was to be subdivided into smaller holdings for settlers to take up.

Thus was laid the foundation of the fruit industry. Like all dreams, when translated into reality, it required a lot of hard work and faith. Orchards do not produce overnight. Each year the orchards required pruning, cultivating, irrigating, and spraying just to bring the trees into produc-

tion. One had to be prepared for several lean years before the rewards could be harvested.

Mistakes were made, often from ignorance of the country and from the tendency to plant unsuitable varieties of fruit. The semi-desert Okanagan could only be made to bloom by the application of irrigation. In spite of this, the idea of fruit production was firmly established.

It was fortunate indeed that among those early orchardists were men of both stubbornness and means. Determined Englishmen and Scots, who were putting down personal roots in the Valley, were set on proving that Kelowna would one day surprise the world with its products. The names of these men are repeated again and again in reports of those early years—Pridham, Crozier, Crichton, Pitcairn, Stirling, Cosens, and, of course, the Rose brothers. There were many others, but these more fortunate families were the ones most able to cope with the early financial costs. They hung in there with determination, and by the turn of the century their efforts were beginning to show results.

In 1908 the dreams of those early fruit farmers would finally become a reality. A board of trade had been formed in 1906 which had thrown itself wholeheartedly into promoting the Kelowna fruit industry. Top priority had been given to advertising the benefits of both the place and its products. Prospective settlers were provided with a comprehensive outline of Kelowna with all its benefits, while potential markets were presented with examples of the fine products of the orchards.

By 1907 the board of trade was advertising throughout the Prairie Provinces. This stirred sufficient interest to have space allocated to the Kelowna fruit industry at the 1908 Calgary Exhibition. F.R.E. DeHart and J. Gibb were sent to Calgary to oversee Kelowna's fruit exhibit. The expertise gained at the Calgary Exhibit was an incentive to enter the Great Spokane Exhibition.

The preceding years had seen more and more orchards in Kelowna producing fruit of high quality. When Kelowna set up its exhibit at Spokane, it proudly proclaimed Kelowna as "The Orchard City," and what an orchard it was!

The Spokane exhibit was a resounding success for Kelowna. Prizes of every description were won. Medals, cups, certificates, substantial amounts of money, and even land deeds were brought home in triumph. Kelowna was firmly "on the map" as the Orchard City.

The board of trade's advertising committee took immediate advantage of these tremendous achievements, and wrote to the agent general of British Columbia asking him to advertise the fruit lands of British Columbia in the *Standard of the Empire*, and to increase the size of the advertising to one-quarter page instead of the former one-eighth. That was just a start. Advertising

for the Okanagan generally, and Kelowna in particular, blossomed forth in many imaginative ways. Every box of fruit shipped had advertising enclosed within. Advertising was placed in newspapers in London and other major cities. A brochure was commissioned, along with the outstanding talents of photographer G.H.E. Hudson, to promote and illustrate the Orchard City.

Meanwhile, in Britain J.S. Redmayne of the British Columbia Information Bu-

reau and Agency was being deluged with enquiries about fruit growing in British Columbia. Certainly it had been given an aura of gentility not only by Lord Aberdeen, who had been appointed governor general to Canada in 1893, but by a later governor general of Canada, Earl Grey, who referred to fruit growing in 1905 as "a beautiful art." In a speech delivered to the Royal Agricultural Society on the occasion of the New Westminster Exhibition in British Columbia he said:

Fruit growing in your Province has acquired the distinction of being a beautiful art as well as a most profitable industry. After a maximum wait of five years, I understand the settler may look forward with reasonable certainty to a net income of $100.00 to $150.00 per acre after all expenses of cultivation have been paid.

Gentlemen, here is a state of things which appears to offer the opportunity of living under such ideal conditions as struggling humanity has only succeeded in reaching in one or two of the most favoured spots upon the earth. There are thousands of families living in England today—families of refinement, culture and distinction, families such as you would welcome among you with both arms—who would be only too glad to come out and occupy a log hut on five acres of a pear or apple orchard in full bearing, if they could do so at reasonable cost.

In reaction to speeches like that, Redmayne obviously had his work cut out to re-

Along with establishing an orchard came daily chores like laundry and cooking. Camping out and living out of a trunk was not unusual for a new landowner in early days. Courtesy, Kelowna Museum Association

spond to all the queries. He decided to write an account of opportunities in British Columbia, and published *Fruit Farming on the Dry Belt of British Columbia* in June 1909. It went into a second printing by September 1909, and a third in 1910. A revised printing with maps was published in 1912. In his preface the author, well aware of the enormous range of enquiries he had to deal with, wrote, with perhaps a little exasperation:

I have endeavoured to set out briefly and without pretence to literary style, what I conceive to be the chief points of information and interest to the Prospective Fruit Settler on the Dry Belt of British Columbia, with the results that what I have to say appears in the form of a somewhat disjointed narrative.

On the other hand, as my object has mainly been to answer those gentlemen who from time to time adress [sic] post card enquiries to me saying "Please tell me all about Fruit Farming on the Dry Belt of British Columbia," but without giving any indication as to their special requirements or the capital they command, I think I may be forgiven if I appear to have treated this fascinating subject too briefly and concisely.

The Orchard City of Kelowna is mentioned frequently by Redmayne, who besides being a wealth of information, believed in "telling it straight," and made no bones about the fact that a young Englishman (or any other prospective orchardist) must come to the area armed with some knowledge. He referred to such young men as "Mud-Pups" and commented, "Respectable individuals do not buy fruit farms in British Columbia for the purpose of training young men from England how to grow fruit on them."

By 1910 the results of the advertising were reflected in the growth of the industry. There were now 31 established fruit growers in Kelowna with paying orchards. There were hundreds of acres of new orchards set out and three fruit-packing plants.

Once again Kelowna took on the world at the Vancouver International Exhibition. Competing against hundreds of entries from many parts of the continent,

This is a splendid example of the displays mounted at international exhibitions. Medals, ribbons, and cups are everywhere, awarded for the fancy and imaginative packing of top grade apples from British Columbia. Courtesy, Kelowna Museum Association

Kelowna reconfirmed its claim to the title "the Orchard City" when a boxcar load of its Jonathan apples won the highest possible award, achieving 1,000 points for the most perfect boxcar of apples ever exhibited.

In 1912-1913, still riding the crest of international recognition, the Kelowna Board of Trade put out a booklet with a wonderful outline of the benefits of living in the Orchard City with the following introduction page:

This Booklet is for the information of those who are looking forward to
establishing a home in a district affording the best conditions for the enjoy-
ment of life. These include a mild, healthful climate, free from the
extremes of cold and heat; pleasant surroundings, congenial neighbors,
and perhaps, most important of all, an occupation at once profit-
able and agreeable. The Board of Trade has nothing to sell,

but desires to place before prospective settlers some of
the more important features that have made Kelowna famous, and also to give in the follow-
ing pages nothing but reliable and trust-
worthy facts. Figures quoted are as
nearly accurate as it is possible
to get them, and readers
may rely on our
statements.

This is followed by 24 pages of excellent information, winding up with a list of "Pertinent Facts in Brief:"

Kelowna is the centre of the finest "dry-belt" fruit lands in British Columbia.
Kelowna has 18,000 acres under cultivation, and 45,000 further available.
Kelowna shipped 400 carloads of fruit and produce in 1911.
Kelowna's population is approximately 2,500.
Kelowna has three Banks, five Churches, two Public Schools, and is now erecting a third which will cost over $60,000 (£12,329). There is also an opera house.
Kelowna won 15 out of 18 first prizes at the Spokane, Was., National Apple Show in 1908.
Kelowna won more prizes than all other British Columbia districts combined at the Spokane Apple Show in 1908.
Kelowna, in 1910, at the Vancouver National Apple Show, won $3,814 (£784), including a $1,000 prize (£206) for the finest carload of apples in the exhibits.
Kelowna's Irrigation Companies spent $700,000 (about £143,836) in two years in development work from 1910 to July, 1912. The total outlay of these great works will approximate $2,000,000 (about £411,000).
Kelowna is about 24 hours from Vancouver and 96 hours from Montreal.
Kelowna is reached, leaving the main line of the C.P.R. at Sicamous, thence South to Okanagan Landing, from there by C.P.R. Steamer.
Kelowna has an up-to-date Light, Power and Water Plant.
Kelowna has a telephone system with rural connec-

tions and long distance phones.
Kelowna is now installing an up-to-date sewage system.
Kelowna has five shipping organizations to facilitate the sale of fruit and produce.
Kelowna has many miles of good roads through the finest scenery in the Okanagan Valley.
The total assessed property valuation for 1912 is $3,000,000 (about £617,000).

Needless to say, this brought in a new flood of enquiries concerning fruit farming.

The fruit-growing industry had other concerns besides setting up exhibits. It was one thing to mount exhibits, but quite another to pack fruit attractively for the general market. It was not long before it was observed that well-packed produce brought better prices. The Horticultural Branch of the Department of Agriculture began to think about establishing packing schools. In Kelowna it was traditional for men only to do the packing.

Redmayne commented that:

Packers are like Poets, they are born and not made. They have a quick mechanical eye and understand and know the different varieties of fruits, and know the colours of the apple they are packing.

A man may become a fairly good packer after six weeks experience. It requires years of experience to be a good packer however, as one must be able to distinguish all varieties of apples, know their size instinctively when they are picked from the pile, and be a good judge of colour. An expert can pack 100 boxes a day.

At about this time a Mrs. Pettman-Gibb, newly widowed with two young sons to support, was desperately seeking work in Kelowna. She applied to the packing houses, but was refused work because of inexperience and because it was not considered "women's work." A lesser woman would have given up, but not this one. She felt she could do the job and set out to prove it. To get a packing school started, there had to be a set number of people not just interested in it, but willing to pay for it. She took her cause to the ladies of the Kelowna Women's Institute. They not only supported her initiative but enrolled themselves in the school, even though the enrollment fee was two dollars each, a fairly steep price in those days, and they did not need the work.

In 1913 it was announced that a Government Fruit Packing School would be started in Kelowna. It seemed that all would be well. Our widow graduated with full qualifications, but could not find a packing house willing to break with tradition and employ her. At last she got work on an "on trial" basis. She shone. She was quick, efficient, and able to keep up with the best of the men. So successful was her "trial" that she was asked to give packing instructions to other women wishing to enter this area of the fruit industry. Since that time, most of the fruit packing in Kelowna has been done by women. The women's liberation movement so applauded in later years was in gear in Kelowna long before it became a cause elsewhere. It was one widow, supported by her sisters at the Women's Institute, who opened the doors of employment for thousands of women.

The whole issue of marketing was one that required considerable planning, particularly for Kelowna. Getting the produce to the consumer was not an easy task given

Stirling and Pitcairn were among the very earliest shippers of Okanagan fruit. They experimented with many types of packs and successfully shipped overseas. Courtesy, Kelowna Museum Association

Above: Seen here second from the left, this woman set the precedent for women packers in the Okanagan Fruit Industry. Courtesy, Kelowna Museum Association

Facing page, top: This truckload of apples is being dispatched from one of Kelowna's many packing houses. There are approximately 350 boxes of apples in the load, with each box containing 40 pounds of apples. Courtesy, Kelowna Museum Association

Facing page, bottom: Tugboats pushed many fruit-bearing barges to the railhead where they were sent off to world markets. The railway transportation of apples has been minimized since refrigerated trucks were developed. Courtesy, Kelowna Museum Association

the geographic location of the valley. In the early 1900s the SS *Aberdeen* worked her way along both shores of Okanagan Lake, picking up boxes of fruit from wharves. With more and more trees coming into production and the Orchard City developing so rapidly, a second sternwheeler was needed. The SS *Okanagan* was launched. The two stern-wheelers and an assortment of work boats were kept busy picking up the fruit and transporting it to the packing houses.

The varieties of fruit planted had to be carefully balanced to ensure a steady flow of fruit. This was particularly true of the apple crop. Apples were, and still are, the main crop. In early days orchardists planned their orchards with a variety of plantings that ripened at different times of the year. Early and late ripeners were important to lengthen the marketing period without producing a glut. No less than 92 varieties of apples have, from time to time, been planted in the Orchard City. Some of the varieties have names that remind one of a "Harlequin Romance" —names like Maidens Blush, Northern Spy, Rob Roy, Duchess of Oldenburg, and Spitzenburg.

After considerable pressure and lobbying an experimental farm was established

to develop strains of fruit adapted to Okanagan conditions, and to investigate ways of utilizing fruit in ways other than in the fresh-fruit market. By 1914, experiments in drying fruit, especially apricots, were showing excellent promise. Many of the apple varieties had weak marketing qualities: some bruised easily; some were not "colour competitive"; others deteriorated too rapidly. With trial and error came success, and certain varieties became the mainstay. Top of the list was the MacIntosh, a true Canadian apple developed by John MacIntosh on his Ontario orchard in the 1800s. Delicious, Jonathans, Winesap, and Golden Delicious were also popular. The Golden Delicious was one of the very few non-red apples that had been accepted by the consuming public. Later varieties were developed at the experimental farm especially for Okanagan production. Among them is the Spartan apple, now becoming popular.

In the early days of Kelowna fruit growing, fruit was packed by individual growers and sales were negotiated in the same way. The packing art having been mastered, the next step was to draw attention to the contents of these beautifully packed boxes. The first of the handmade wooden boxes often had as decoration only a simple stamped-on message to kindly return the box to the Kelowna Growers Exchange. As more orchards competed for the market, other methods of identifying the growers were developed. It is not certain when fruit labels were first created for the box ends, but certainly it was quite early in the game. Some were quite simple, while others developed into beautiful or exotic illustrations depicting everything from an immaculately laid out orchard to the thistle brand of McDougalls Export Company.

By 1914 the Okanagan needed yet a

third stern-wheeler, and the SS *Sicamous* was launched.

Poised on the edge of even more development, Kelowna was suddenly depleted of many of its menfolk. War had come, and many of the English and Scots settlers had strong ties to regiments that had been part of their family traditions for generations. The Orchard City, the western Garden of Eden, was left in the care of the women and old folk while the image of the orchards, lake, and blue sky was carried in the hearts of the men at the front. The Orchard City of Kelowna settled into a period of waiting, and coping. Much of the development money was tied up in Britain and Europe, and it was many years before further expansion could be resumed.

In the preceding 20 years the land had been transformed from open range and timberland to hundreds of acres of bearing fruit trees. Kelowna was, without a doubt, an Orchard City.

This picture is unusual in that a conscious effort has been made to reflect the multicultural heritage of Canada. The Victory Bond drive was outstandingly successful in Kelowna. Courtesy, Kelowna Museum Association

4

Headaches and Heartbreak

Kelowna, tucked away between the mountains, has never been a victim of major natural devastation. There are, from time to time, occasions when an icy finger of cold coming down from the north causes an exceptionally unpleasant winter of frozen lakes and general discomfort. Or, more of a problem, a heavy fall of snow in the hills, melting too quickly, might cause spring flooding. A few times dishes have been rattled in cupboards because of a minor earth tremor but, on the whole, Kelowna has been free of intensely violent natural phenomena.

The distress and heartache experienced by Kelowna settlers has been, for the most part, man-made.

Kelowna's earliest white settlers, full of optimism and ready to work hard, were all transplants. While they set down new roots, there was that corner of the heart that would never be completely won by the New World. Homesickness and yearning were personal battles often fought and not always won. Some returned and sank thankfully back into the familiar ways of their motherland.

To this love of homeland was added inherent loyalty to the sovereign. To fight for King and Country, wherever the arena happened to be, was something one did without question.

The Boer War of 1899 was the first to call on this allegiance. War at this time in history still had an aura of first-hand adventure and the challenge of meeting the foe face to face. The idea of riding in a cavalry charge with swords and lances at the ready was an irresistible lure for many young men. A number of Kelowna's rather scant population volunteered their services. The soldiers were sent off with much ceremony and good wishes, and also among well-hidden forebodings of what might be the outcome of this deadly adventure. Fortunately this war was of comparatively short duration, lasting from October 1899 until May 1902. When the Kelowna men returned they were welcomed and cheered through a specially constructed Victory Arch set up near the boat wharf.

Life settled back into the routine of getting the orchards into production. Between 1908 and 1912 the fruit industry prospered.

Then again a faraway situation began to touch the Okanagan. Europe was moving closer to the brink of war, and this froze both people and money resources. Development of the West was dependent on outside sources for both of these commodities. The people moving westward to the Prairie Provinces provided one of the biggest markets for the fruit produced. By 1913 there was only a trickle of people coming in to settle. Markets began to decline. To add to the problem, money committed for development was suddenly frozen. Much of this cash flow had been pledged from British and Belgian sources. Businessmen in Kelowna had put their own futures on the line by signing obligations for development, based on promises of money to come. With the outbreak of war came financial disaster. The people who had signed guarantees with the bank, especially with land and irrigation developments, were now faced with meeting the obligations.

It was a truly terrible situation. For many, everything they owned was tied up in the orchards or land. Faced with declining markets, the orchardists saw their incomes dwindle. Without the money committed from Britain and Belgium to help pay the bills, land developers were left to deal with the costs incurred from subdividing and installing irrigation systems on land that had no potential buyers.

On paper, this is just one more small piece of history, but to the people involved it left indelible scars. Many families in Kelowna lived on the edge of poverty and uncertainty for years. William Carruthers, the son of one of these guarantors, said in his later years, "As a boy, I hated that Bank. Every penny we had went to 'The Bank.' We never could afford to do anything or go anywhere. All my life I have hated that Bank, and to this time I will not do business with them. They stole my boyhood."

Even though no money could be expected from the sale of crops, orchardists could not calmly put their orchards aside. Fruit farming, unlike some other types of farming, simply doesn't work that way. A cattleman can reduce his herd, a grain farmer can plant less land, but a tree needs attention *every* year. The choice for orchardists was a sort of "all or nothing" situation. Five years of hard work and investment could be lost with one year of neglect.

So the trees were pruned, irrigated, and sprayed, and in due course produced yet another unsalable harvest.

The declaration of World War I did not change any of these problems. It simply added another, this one so charged with emotional decisions that other problems were momentarily eclipsed.

The call from King and Country to take up arms could not be ignored. The men of Kelowna responded, and fathers, sons, husbands, and brothers rallied to "do their duty." Although the Okanagan Valley population was not heavy at this time, 1,000 volunteers in the immediate area were sent off at one time on the SS *Sicamous*. The city sent them off proudly in 1916. A large banner was hung on the deck of the boat proclaiming "Kelowna's Gift of 1,000 Men." This gift consisted of fresh-faced young men going off to the great adventure; middle-aged men, some of whom

held commissions in "family" regiments; glory seekers; and escapists. Almost everyone left behind a family—torn between grief and pride at giving up a loved one. Those left behind turned to the task of "keeping the home fires burning," a task now doubly hard with the strength of the men away.

Those eager adventurers on the SS *Sicamous* soon found that the glory of war was often translated into defending or taking a foxhole of small dimensions on the bloody battlefields of France. Canadians played a large and unforgettable role in assaulting places like Vimy Ridge. Most of these soldiers and their families had

never heard of such a place prior to this time. The Battle of Vimy Ridge was a Canadian-fought battle, and was the greatest victory of the war up to that time. That victory cost 3,598 lives. This was followed by two more outstanding Canadian battles, the Somme and the Passchendaele, the latter resulting in 15,654 Canadian casualties. A report from a Passchendaele stretcher party seemed to sum up the whole scene of horror and futility. The stretcher-bearers stumbled over two bodies, one Canadian, one German, grappling still in death. They had fought desperately and, sucked into the swampy ground, had died in one another's arms.

"Kelowna's Gift of 1,000 Men" left for service during World War I aboard the SS *Sicamous*. It is seen here pulling away from the Kelowna wharf in 1916. Courtesy, Kelowna Museum Association

They could not be separated, so were buried together.

There was hardly a town in Canada that escaped the dreaded telegrams bringing the feared news and adding to the growing list of newly made widows and fatherless children.

Parents received a few personal odds and ends and a military tag, all that was left of a beloved son. Usually these were accompanied by a letter from a commanding officer, commending their son for bravery and assuring them he had not suffered. Such a letter was received by the mother of Sergeant L.A. (Len) McMillan of Kelowna which says in part:

I regret very much to have to report to you, the death, in action, of your son. At the time of his death he was taking part in the great advance. You will be glad to know that his death was instantaneous, so he did not suffer.
Your son was one of the best leaders in our company. He earned an enviable reputation amongst both officers and men.

Kelowna had sent more men to war per capita than even most English communities. There the highest ratio was 237 per 10,000 population. Kelowna had sent more than 200 from an area population of 6,000 and still more were going daily. A long list in the Kelowna newspaper listed another 75 volunteers in 1917. Among them were two Raymers, two Sutherlands, and a Gillard.

It was during the desperate fighting in France that two Canadians put their emotions into words, so movingly and eloquently, that today are world-renown. Many have read and have been moved by the lines written by John McCrae:

In Flanders Fields the Poppies blow
Between the crosses, row on row.

The Battle of Passchendaele was in Flanders.

At about the same time Robert Service, known for his "Ballad of Dangerous Dan McGrew," was a stretcher-bearer, and wrote *Rhymes of a Red Cross Man.* In them is reflected the horror of broken bodies that were all around him.

Hasten, Oh God! Thy Night!
Hide from my eyes the sight
of the body I stare and see
shattered so hideously
I can't believe that it's mine.

In Kelowna the papers published lists of the dead and wounded. Headlines such as "Two More Local Boys Fall in Battle" were common.

At the same time the government was exhorting those at home to produce food and supplies for overseas troops. The women of Kelowna planted gardens, tended the orchards, rolled bandages, and bought and sold Victory Bonds.

A committee was formed to facilitate the sending of a carload of apples to "the boys overseas." The packing houses supplied and packed the fruit free of charge.

Mercifully the war finally ended. An armistice was signed and the boys came home. For those who did not come home, the Kelowna War Memorial was dedicated on August 7, 1921. Among the officiating clergy was the Venerable Archdeacon ("Daddy") Greene. There are 134 names carved into the memorial. Nine families had lost two of their loved ones, and the McMillan family lost three. Vimy Ridge had taken a number of Kelowna men. Survivors of that terrible battle have each year since gathered at the Kelowna Branch of the Royal Canadian Legion for Vimy Night Remembrances. Each year the number grows smaller, but like the survivors of Agincourt, as Shakespeare says, "They remember with advantages" the days of fighting at Vimy.

Immediately after the war, not a great deal changed in Kelowna, but men had fought for a better world and had expectations to find it. They came back to their orchards and set about marketing their products.

Just prior to the war—in the face of dwindling markets, foreign competition, and independent attempts at marketing—the Okanagan United Fruit Growers had been formed. This group, established in 1913, brought together several packing houses to market through a single office. Through diligent effort and expanding production the Okanagan fruit industry was able to penetrate the Prairie markets again. By 1915 it had approximately 39 percent of the apple market in those provinces. The return of the men and a new flow of optimism and settlers brought that percentage steadily up.

Not all the war veterans, however eager, were permitted to take over producing orchards. It was felt that orchards should be left in the hands of those with orchard "know-how," and not turned over to inexperienced men.

All the experience in the valley would not have been enough to keep things going as 1919 came along. In that year many other traditional fruit suppliers had produced small crops, leaving a need in the marketplace. Kelowna was able to take advantage of the market demand, because the trees planted since 1910 were beginning to produce large crops. But this soon created problems. There was considerable difficulty in getting the fruit transported to the markets. The packing houses were congested and pleas were made to the CPR to put on more boxcars. This problem was somewhat alleviated

when the railway announced it would provide an additional 500 boxcars.

In 1920 the Okanagan apple crop was 1,317,000 boxes. In 1921 it had jumped to an incredible 2,769,000 boxes. Unable to absorb this phenomenal amount, the market began to fail in 1922. The only thing that kept growers from catastrophe was that the crop in the United States was small and could not compete for the Prairie markets. Panic did strike, however, as growers tried desperately to market their fruit. The result was a plunge in Prairie prices as growers tried to undercut one another.

By the following year the growers realized the full impact of the situation. It became clear that a new marketing policy had to be adopted.

They held meetings and invited speakers of experience to detail the benefits of such a course. Aaron Sapiro, a successful organizer of cooperative-marketing agencies, stated:

Cooperative marketing means the substitution of merchandising for dumping. Here apple growers just dumped their apples on consignment. In 1922 for example they got scared because they had so many apples, rushed them to shippers, who in turn besieged jobbers with offers of Okanagan apples. The Okanagan growers were themselves to blame for disastrous prices last season, they themselves broke the market.

After considering their situation, many growers signed up to market through a cooperative with a single selling office. But their problems were not to be solved so simply.

This was the beginning of a long rollercoaster ride in the fruit industry. The growers hung on grimly, seeing prices decline year after year. Every so often there was an optimistic little upswing, but far more often there were not enough markets for the ever-increasing crops. Pleas to the government produced a good deal of "buck passing" but no tangible results until 1927, when the Produce Marketing Act was passed. Hope rose again, only to be dashed in 1928 with a crop that broke all records and put an excessive strain on the newly formed market committee. It was in this sorry state that the Depression hit, and buying power everywhere was reduced even more. By 1932 most growers had suffered losses on their crops. In one instance a shipper received only 20 cents a box for apples that had cost him a minimum of 33 cents to produce. Worse was to follow in 1933. In a cost-cutting exercise, the provincial government decided, in this of all years, to suspend the annual grant that the fruit-marketing body depended on.

Disturbed and angry at the prospect of total and utter ruin, the growers of Kelowna and district held a meeting on September 4. A resolution was prepared and another meeting called for September 5. The resolution read:

The growers' present position is due to the consignment of fruit to the Packing Houses. Therefore, be it resolved; that the growers organize and refuse to deliver fruit to the packing houses unless the shippers guarantee not to pack or ship such fruit unless it brings a minimum of one cent a pound.

The growers were on strike. "A cent a pound, or on the ground" was their fighting slogan.

They knew this resolution would be of no consequence unless they could monitor movement of fruit from the less-militant orchardists who would try to supply the packing houses. Pickets were set up on the bridges of the main roads leading into Kelowna from the orchard areas. Un-less the driver of the truck or wagon could produce a written statement from the prospective shipper that a cent a pound would be forthcoming, the wagons and trucks were turned back and unloaded.

The outcome was the formation of a stabilization board to set prices. A minimum of a cent a pound was agreed on and shippers were to make part payment within a month of shipping. Again, not every shipper wished to belong to this arrangement but finally all 52 fruit shippers in the valley joined.

It was not long before some of the shippers wanted, for various reasons, to opt out. This would in effect put everyone back to square one. The orchardists were not prepared to have this happen. When it was discovered that bulk apples from one shipper were being loaded onto boxcars in contravention of the agreement, a mass rally was called. It was decided that this shipment must be stopped at all costs. The crowd, consisting of 400 growers, their wives, and their children, surged onto the railway tracks at Kelowna and placed themselves between the boxcars and the locomotive, declaring the only way the two would meet was over their dead bodies. Fortunately such a sacrifice was not levied. The train crew wanted no part of the dispute and attended to other duties. To make sure the boxcars stayed put, the crowd stayed until 2:30 P.M., at which time word was received that legal action had been executed to keep the boxcars from being moved. Before the hearings were held, the rebel shippers agreed to abide by the original agreement and the stabilization board won the day. It was by no means the end of the problem. Marketing, although now more orderly, was more or less a crisis situation from year to year, and went through many forms of controlled selling and shipping organizations.

Rather than dump excess fruit, growers tried to find ways of getting it to the depressed Provinces. Many carloads of fruit were freely distributed, and when times improved the Prairie People showed their gratitude by reopening markets with their British Columbia friends. Courtesy, Kelowna Museum Association

Throughout all of this one would think that Kelowna orchardists would have little time or compassion for problems in other places. Such was not the case. During the Depression, carloads of apples were sent to hard-hit cities on the Prairies to be distributed free of charge.

Kelowna saw its share of drifters throughout the Depression. One old-timer recalled that every morning one summer his mother made large stacks of thick cucumber sandwiches to hand out to the hungry men and boys that stopped by. These drifters sought any odd job in exchange for food. He recalled that was one summer he didn't have to split any wood. All had been done by these hungry drifters.

By early 1937 there were a few glimmers of prospective markets. The February 11 issue of the *Courier* had the welcome headline: "Boom on Apple Sales with Rise in Temperature." This news item followed:

After more than a month of desultory trading, the prairie markets opened up this week and flooded the Okanagan with orders for apples. Movement was brisk on Tuesday and by Wednesday the improvement was decidedly marked. McIntosh are nearly cleaned up, the Spies are beginning to move, and Romes are now moving freely. Figures for the week ending February 6, as released last evening by the B.C. Fruit Board, showed that 28,749 boxes of apples were shipped domestic and 6,079 boxes export in that time. This brings the balance unsold in the entire area to roughly 233,000 boxes.

Finally, in 1937, the minister of agriculture presented to the government the Natural Products Marketing Act to introduce

"A scheme to control and regulate the Transportation, Packing, Storage, and Marketing of British Columbia Tree Fruits."

While peace was being achieved in the fruit industry, across the sea it was a different story.

In 1939, when war broke out in Europe, the patterns in Canadian attitude towards previous wars were repeated. Certainly in some areas of Canada the urge to respond was perhaps not quite as strong, but Kelownans were still, for the most part, of British ancestry. To them there was no question about going. Often the only queries were: "Am I old enough?" "Can I volunteer?" "Will I be accepted?"

Many young men wished to join British Columbia's own regiment, the British Columbia Dragoons. Service in the Royal Canadian Air Force also enticed prospective enlistees. Commando and paratroop activities had strong appeal because of their

special tasks and training. Some sought adventure on the seas in the Canadian Merchant Navy, supplying Britain with supplies and trusting to luck that a U-boat did not detect their presence.

The Okanagan is represented in the Canadian navy by two vessels: the submarine *Okanagan* (one of three sister submarines named for Indian groups whose name started with an "O") and the HMCS *Kelowna,* a corvette. During the war, the crew of the *Kelowna* exchanged letters and gifts with residents of Kelowna.

Thousands of Canadian troops were sent to Britain on almost anything that would float. Few single vessels had the luxury of an escort, and even convoys with a warship in attendance were not assured of safe conduct.

In Britain the Canadians were further trained and readied for the day of invasion. Prior to that event a mini-invasion was mounted. Canadians played a major

role in this exercise. The Dieppe raid on the coast of France is still being debated. Was it a success or failure? The one sure thing is that it cost many Canadians their lives. The commander-in-chief of the Second Division of Canadian Forces Overseas was Major General R.F.L. Keller, C.B.E. Croix de guerre, who was born and raised in Kelowna, son of an early Kelowna doctor.

From Britain, Canadian forces went to all fronts: to Italy, Sicily, Libya, and, after the invasion, throughout Europe. Some even went on to Burma.

Canadians have a special place in the hearts and memories of the people of the Netherlands. To the British Columbia Dragoons went the honour of leading the liberating forces into many Dutch cities. Tulips from Holland grow in Kelowna's city park, a gift from the people of the Netherlands. Because of the efforts of the British Columbia Dragoons (whose headquarters are in

the Okanagan) and the citizens of Veendam in the Netherlands, Kelowna and Veendam are sister cities.

Les Kerry of the *Capital News* in Kelowna received many letters from servicemen and servicewomen overseas, in
response to ones written by him. Some of
them were very thoughtful. One men-
tions that returning servicemen were going to want more from the future than
had been offered to their fathers after
World War I. Memories of the hungry
'30s were obviously apparent. Another
says feelingly, ". . . if ever I get back to Kelowna I will never again complain about
mud in the orchards at pruning time. The
mud we have lived in over here [the Ital-
ian front] has to be seen to be believed."

Kelowna lost many of its young in
the war, and at war's end the bereaved families set about creating a special remem-
brance. As most of the young men and
women had been brought up with the
love of sports and the concept of fair
play, and had had the opportunity to
skate on outside ponds, it was decided
that a sports arena, to include an ice surface, would be appropriate. In 1945 the Kelowna Memorial Arena was built.

One postwar development was a realization that Kelowna must somehow expand
its income base. To do this it needed to
be less isolated. More people and a diversity of business were needed. The sawmill
and the fruit industry were still the largest employers, along with other agricultural ventures such as chicken and turkey
farms, mink and chinchilla ranches, and a
budding wine-making industry. It was
still a small town where one greeted
one's neighbors and everyone knew almost everybody.

The provincial government decided a
road was needed to connect the Okanagan to the rest of the province. The Hope-

Princeton highway was completed in
1949. This passed through the mountain-
ous area separating the valley from the
coast. Canyons and steep grades made construction difficult, but the effort was accom-
plished.

Completion of the Hope-Princeton highway increased the population. Between
1949 and 1959 travellers "discovered" the
beautiful city of Kelowna by the lake. Kelowna's population doubled and building increased. The fruit industry saw some of
its most prosperous years, marred unfortu-
nately by several major packing-house
fires. These occurred so close together
that there was a suspicion of arson and
an attempt to cripple the marketing ability of the industry.

Gradually it was realized that tourists
brought in money. New service industries
opened in response to this new market.

Tourists coming in over the Hope-
Princeton road were still bottlenecked
when they reached Okanagan Lake. The
three ferries in service were strained to
the limit. It was with a sinking heart that
a driver nearing the ferry wharf saw cars approaching. This meant that a ferry had
just been in and this was the traffic from
it. There would a 20-minute wait (at least)
for the next one. So it was with great joy
and celebration that the news was hailed
that a bridge was to be built. This floating bridge—almost a mile long and composed of pontoons, with a lift span for
boat traffic to pass under—was opened in
1958.

Kelowna's small-town days were numbered. Finally the last step to opening the
valley was taken. This was the building of
Rogers Pass, which opened the route to
the Prairie Provinces. Almost immediately
people from Alberta, Saskatchewan, and Manitoba discovered the Okanagan, with its
milder winters and its acres of orchards

and the sparkling blue Okanagan Lake. Compared to Prairie winters, Kelowna seemed a little bit of heaven.

The lake, ever since the townsite was laid out, had always played a significant part in Kelowna development. This did not apply only to commerce. It was a natural playground. In the early days the lake was the scene of family outings and picnics. From these informal get-togethers came the idea for an annual event. The first Kelowna Regatta was held in 1906. This consisted of canoe and boat races, swimming, diving, and other water-oriented events. Soon competition with other towns in the Okanagan began. In time, towns as far away as Vancouver (even before the road link) came to the annual event.

It grew. Night shows with headline performers and synchronized-swimming teams were added. Now it had the title of

the Kelowna International Regatta. One day of events grew to two, then three, then almost a whole week.

With the growth of the regatta came problems. The population doubled during the event with the influx of visitors and participants. This in turn required more policing, garbage monitoring, parking, and accommodations. Kelowna managed to keep on top of all these things, and continued to seek new ways of entertaining the expectant crowds. The stadium was enlarged to seat more people, and an aura of fun and good will was still the dominant mood.

The first real disaster of the regatta celebration happened on June 13, 1969. The 13th certainly was a bad luck date. The stadium—the main facility of the regatta—was destroyed beyond hope of salvage by a spectacular fire. Huge billows of smoke rolled up into the air and could

Left: Mayor Dick Parkinson (left) is seen here with the 1963 Lady of the Lake. Each year the Regatta adopted a different theme and Honour City. In 1963 Edmonton was so honoured. Courtesy, Kelowna Museum Association

Below: The Blue Angels, Golden Hawks, and Snow Birds have all performed at the Regatta, with the lake and hills providing a splendid setting for the air shows. Courtesy, Kelowna Museum Association

be seen for miles. Flames shot forth with intense heat. Although there was water in plenty from the nearby lake, it was impossible to douse the roaring fire. The blaze was believed to have been caused by a couple of young boys, smoking their first cigarettes. They had tucked themselves away out of sight in the lowest part of the building for the experiment. The fire presented an enormous problem to the regatta committee as to whether the event could be held that year. It was scheduled for August and, incredibly, it did indeed take place on schedule.

Among the new entertainment added to the regatta were the air shows. These proved to be very successful. Watching the breathtaking dives, the symmetrical flying formations, and the speed and skill of the aerial acrobats was thrilling. All heads turned as if attached by string to watch the planes come zooming past and, in seconds, climb up and over the hills out of sight. The pilots, ever-willing to give the best of all possible performances, manoeuvred their planes magnificently.

In 1969 the Blue Angels were the featured planes. They gave a never-to-be-forgotten performance. One of the pilots, caught up in the thrill of the moment, broke the sound barrier. Along with this resounding thunderclap of noise came the tinkling of thousands of pieces of falling glass—all that was left of the store windows in downtown Kelowna. In a several-block radius, hardly a window was left intact. In spite of the fact that Kelowna was packed with visitors, mercifully the casualties were few. Cuts were the worst of the injuries. The stunned store owners strove to board up their premises and clear away the broken spear-like shards of glass. This could have been a catastrophe of major proportions had the blast occurred an hour or two earlier, as the

streets were lined with crowds awaiting the parade.

Not so fortunate was the air event of the skydivers. The plane flew over the stands and the brightly dressed skydivers jumped out, aiming to land in the city park. One by one the parachutes popped open. Onlookers watched in horror as one of the descending divers hurtled closer and closer earthward. The speeding body disappeared from view, parachute still unopened. The tragic result was found a short time later in a Kelowna alleyway.

The fire, the broken sound barrier, and the death of the skydiver all left their marks on the regatta festivities.

In spite of everything, Kelowna had been celebrating a regatta for more than 80 years when the 1986 celebration was scheduled. Parades, bands, an air show, and all the water events were organized and Kelowna looked forward to another gala affair. But this was to be the "Year of the Hooligan."

Saturday night, July 26, 1986, came and with it a gathering of youths out for excitement. The mood grew, and the stage was set for violence to break out. Who knows what triggers a riot? Whatever it is, it was present that night. Singing and chanting began. The police force grew uneasy. A rock was thrown and then another. The riot beast was unleashed. Hundreds of young men and women suddenly gave in to primitive impulses. They hurled bottles, rocks, anything they could throw, through windows, on cars, and at each other and the police force. Reserve peacekeepers were called out as the battle grew in intensity. In the early hours of Sunday morning the mayor was obliged to read the Riot Act.

Kelowna was in a state of bewilderment as dawn came on Sunday. Shopkeep-

RED BIRD
OF KELOWNA.

ers looked with dismay at broken windows and looted stores. The council, regatta officials, and the citizens of Kelowna could not believe this had happened in their beautiful city. It was a black year for the regatta.

As the 1987 regatta was planned, many safeguards were considered and vigilance was stressed. Nevertheless 1987 was the most painful year in the history of the Kelowna Regatta. From all parts of the province and beyond came the thrill seekers. They came with rocks and clubs in the trunks of their cars. They came with intent.

As Saturday evening grew close, the knots of agitators began to prepare for business. What did they care that they were about to disrupt a city and an 80-year tradition? With a few drinks to make it all seem right, the fight was on. Bottles, bricks, and rocks flew again. If Kelowna had been stunned before, the city was in utter shock that this could be happening again. For the second time the Riot Act was read. A number of the ringleaders were arrested. The concen-

trated efforts of the vastly outnumbered police managed to divert the mob away from the downtown area, thus minimizing the damage, although window breaking and looting was considerable.

If ever there was heartbreak and headache combined, this was it. Should the regatta be abandoned? Was the friendly and popular tradition of 80 years to be brought to an end? As Kelowna entered 1988 these questions were examined. The people of the city decided that there would not be a regatta.

Kelowna pride—something that two world wars and a Depression couldn't kill—has been tested by the lawlessness of a few. A new attempt to strengthen pride in the city has been mounted, with the formation of the Kelowna Pride Committee. Perhaps a large growing city cannot keep the home-town flavour of the past, and, sadly, will have to trade in this long-standing tradition. But the Kelowna Pride Committee is working hard to preserve the best of the old spirit and combine it with the city's new status.

In 1906 Kelowna held what was to be the first of the Kelowna Regattas. This event grew to become the single most important event in Kelowna. The earliest Regattas were a wonderful experience for the whole family. They were so popular that they quickly became the highlight of the summer. Courtesy, Kelowna Museum Association

The Okanagan Players travelled the Province with their offerings and received acclaim wherever they went. They set a standard that Kelowna performers have strived to maintain. The quality of the sets and costumes shown here gives some idea of the care that went into the productions. Courtesy, Kelowna Museum

5

On the Rebound

If a competition was ever held concerning the most controversial and talked about character of the Okanagan, Ogopogo would surely be the winner.

Ogopogo, the monster of the lake, known to the Indians as "N'haitik," has made regular appearances since earliest times. Like his cousin the Loch Ness monster, Ogopogo has been the object of every kind of investigation. Pictures, sketches, movie footage of blurry objects, and reputable people swearing to the validity of their statements abound. A substantial reward has been offered for proof positive, but Ogopogo remains as aloof and mysterious as ever.

His present name comes from a music-hall ditty about a creature whose "mother was an earwig and whose father was a whale," and whose name was Ogopogo. In 1924 this song inspired some humourist to apply the name to the oft-spotted lake monster, who seemed to have no name (except the little-known Indian one) and could hardly be called "that thing" indefinitely. With the christening a spate of sightings occurred, and Ogopogo was regarded as a possible menace to lake traffic. This reached such a pitch that when a new ferry was being constructed in 1926, it was announced that it would be armed with "monster repelling devices."

Legend has it that Ogopogo lives in a cave in the deepest part of the lake in an area known as Squally Point. Indian travellers crossing the lake in their canoes, or especially when swimming their horses across, always took along a small gift to appease the monster should he appear.

Many theories have been advanced for and against Ogopogo's existence. The lake is deep and long, and so far no proof either way has been forthcoming. Could so many earnest and truthful people be mistaken? The mystery continues and Ogopogo sightings are reported regularly. He is our resident celebrity.

Every so often Ogopogo is eclipsed by the arrival of other celebrities. Kelowna has had its share of visits from "greats." The first of these were the Earl and Countess of Aberdeen, the motivating forces in establishing commercial fruit growing in Kelowna. Probably it was

When Rembler Paul and his wife died they were buried in this tomb, carefully prepared in advance by Rembler. Its location is known to only a few, and currently the only visible portion is one corner. Rembler and his wife lie undisturbed, exactly as he would have wished. Courtesy, Kelowna Museum Association

their influence that enticed others in their society to come to Kelowna. Since Kelowna was not on a main line between major points, the city had to be a planned destination for illustrious visitors and not just part of a general itinerary. Famous people came to Kelowna because they wished to, not by accident.

Sometimes infamous people came here too. This was the case when Bill Miner, the man on which the movie *The Silver Fox* was based, came to Kelowna in 1905. He is credited with first using the now-famous order "hands up." Fortunately for Kelowna there did not seem to be any great attraction here for Miner, and he went on his way without using his famous phrase.

More than a few eccentrics came our way, among them Remblar Paul. Wanting to be secure when he went to his last resting place, Paul built a concrete tomb into the mountainside and installed a

heavy reinforced steel door at the entrance. Here Paul and his wife lie undisturbed. An article in a popular magazine described it as one of the six most difficult places to break into in Canada. The tomb is presently covered with gravel with just one corner visible, a precaution against macabre vandalism.

In earlier times travel was considered necessary to broaden one's education. Many people of means went on the "Grand Tour." As new country opened up it too became part of "the tour." Most of these types of travellers obviously expected there would be "proper" accommodation. The railways did their best to provide this with wonderful buildings like the Banff Springs Hotel in the Rockies and similar grand accommodation adjacent to the line. The closest hotel of this kind for Kelowna was at Sicamous where the railway passed closest to the Okanagan. From there one went to the head of the lake and took the stern-wheeler.

Among the visitors was Countess Bubna. She was typical of many wealthy travellers and on arrival in Kelowna was shocked at what she considered totally inadequate hotel facilities. In spite of this the country attracted her and she invested in land. The thought that her social equals might possibly look down their noses at Kelowna obviously rankled her. There *would* be a proper hotel, even if she had to finance one—which she did. This was the Eldorado Arms, built in 1926. It was a large Tudor-style building set in an English garden overlooking Okanagan Lake. Three windows with family coat of arms in stained glass were features of the hotel. A gracious stairway led off from a large wood-panelled lounge furnished in fine oak and with oil paintings on the walls. This became the mecca for all well-to-do travellers, while the Lake-

view, the Royal, and the Palace hotels housed less-illustrious travellers. The register of the Lakeview shows that it had its "regulars," probably salesmen.

There was a great interest in all the goings-on in Kelowna. Like in all small communities, gossip and rumour added a little spice to otherwise routine lives. A column in the *Courier* headed "Items of Interest" gave good coverage of all the city's events, from Miss Jones' broken ankle (often followed up by a progress on her recovery) to the flower-show winner, to a new paint job on a house or store.

All the comings and goings were tied to the stern-wheelers. They carried in all travellers, mail, and merchandise, and took out all that was departing. Meeting the boat was the highlight of the day. The dock was the scene of countless ceremonies. One of the more exuberant ones was in March 1913 when a resounding send-off was given to 20 Chinese men as they boarded the boat to go off to lay steel for the Kettle Valley Railway. Most of Kelowna's Chinese community were there to see them off.

The stern-wheelers had some quite illustrious travellers, including royalty. One can imagine the pitch of excitement in 1919 when it was learned the future King

of England, Edward, Prince of Wales, might travel to Kelowna. On September 30 of that year a cavalcade of cars drove up the valley from Vernon escorting the Prince into Kelowna.

The *Kelowna Record* reported, "With a crowd such as has probably never been seen in the city before, Kelowna welcomed the visiting Prince of Wales." In his welcoming speech the mayor managed to plug the city, saying:

Kelowna, known throughout this western land as the Orchard City of British Columbia, is the centre of an agricultural district of which we believe we have just cause to be extremely proud. We venture to believe that you will be interested to know that our fruit goes into many of the world's greatest markets. To China, South America, South Africa, Australia and New Zealand, and also in London where they have won the highest possible diplomas!

It is reported that the Prince answered in a clear voice, saying in part, "I have heard much of the agricultural wealth of this district, and I also know of your splendid services during the Great War."

He then received several boxes of apples which had been especially packed by

all the packing houses as a gift to Her Majesty the Queen. The apples apparently were received by the Queen in good order as a letter of thanks was sent from Buckingham Palace on November 19, 1919, to the mayor.

After the ceremonies the Prince was conducted to the SS *Sicamous*, where those sending him off waved until "the boyish figure of the Prince could no longer be distinguished." The Prince was a great favourite of the people, and in later years they would agonize with him as he wrestled with the problem of abdicating or giving up "the woman he loved."

The year 1919 was a busy one for Kelowna. The Prince had barely left before the viceroyal party of his excellency the governor general of Canada, the Duchess of Devonshire, and her daughter Lady Do-

rothy Cavendish, arrived. On October 9 the wharf was crowded with cheering children as the party stepped off the boat. During his stop, the Duke made presentations of medals won in the war. This had been scheduled for the Prince's visit, but the medals had not been received in time. The Duke toured the tobacco shed being operated by Louis Holman and expressed great interest in the industry.

Along with all the fanfare, Kelowna experienced important growth in the early 1900s, particularly in health care.

Since the early days of settlement, Kelownans had realized that they would need a good medical man. Dr. Benjamin De-Furlong Boyce filled this role in the late 1800s. He covered an astonishing amount of territory. As Dr. Boyce was the only

Kelowna's Tug-O-War team is seen here with one of their many trophies. "Big" Sam Elliot is seated on the right, a perfect anchorman. Courtesy, Kelowna Museum Association

doctor in the area for several years, the majority of settlers relied on home remedies for everyday aches and pains, as often the doctor would be a two-day ride away at the "other end" of his practice. Great reliance therefore was put on the *Home Medicine Book,* of which there were many versions. In many there were wonderful illustrations of rashes that could be used for diagnosis.

Dr. Boyce, like his associates, made all his rounds on horseback or horse and buggy. With the advent of the motor car, Dr. Boyce was able to indulge his "gentleman" image with the purchase of a sleek Napier. This was the most extravagant mode of transportation Kelowna had ever seen.

In 1908 the Kelowna Cottage Hospital was opened with much ceremony. Dr. Boyce assisted in the event.

Soon there were more doctors to call on, notably Dr. Herman Keller and Dr. William John Knox. The latter would become the deliverer of hundreds of Kelowna babies, and a much-loved physician. Dr. Knox worked hard for public health. He regularly submitted medical reports for all the schools in the growing school district. He was among the first to urge the use of iodized salt to help combat the number of thyroid conditions that he observed.

The modest hospital grew apace. A nurses residence was built, and over the years the hospital has been further expanded. Today it is considered one of the best hospitals in British Columbia, with an excellent medical staff and board who constantly strive to provide Kelowna with the very best in equipment.

Canadians seem to have influenced public health in other parts of the world, particularly China. Prior to becoming Kelowna's first dentist, Dr. William J.N. Sheppard had spent a number of years in China setting up a series of public dental clinics. His work must have had some significance as among his treasures was counted a beautiful Chinese robe on which is embroidered the "royal dragons." These are dragons exhibiting five toes per foot, and can only be worn or approved by the royal house. All others wear four-toed dragons. Dr. Sheppard's robe was probably presented to him as a token of royal esteem. It is now part of the Kelowna Museum's collections.

As the years passed, Kelowna residents added many improvements to their city. Electric light came to downtown Kelowna quite early; by 1909 a small powerhouse was in place.

Above: Benjamin De-Furlong Boyce came to the area in 1894. A noted doctor, he served the entire area first on horse, by horse and buggy, and finally by motor car. He participated in much of Kelowna's social and sporting life. Courtesy, Kelowna Museum Association

Right: These nurses are seen here outside the Nurses Residence in Kelowna. The standards for nurses trained here were exceptionally high. For many it was a lifelong commitment, which included making home-care visits, as well as performing many hospital duties. Courtesy, Kelowna Museum Association

A rather sad item was reported on December 18, 1919, which said:

An old timer of the Kelowna District and one who had done many years faithful service in humble capacity, died yesterday. He was the old Pinto horse which had been hauling the slabs and sawdust into the power house ever since there was a power house. He was an old timer when he started that useful occupation and his age is wrapt in mystery. He died in harness, dropping over quietly whilst doing his duty.

Country folk still relied on kerosene lamps for illumination, and later pump-up gas lamps were used. It was quite a dazzling spectacle for out-of-towners to come into the brightly lit shopping centre of Kelowna. Some of the outlying areas did not get electricity until the 1940s.

All in all 1919 was a historic year. November 29 saw the grand opening of the Empress Theatre. The movies had come to

Kelowna. They opened with a triple bill: *Mickey,* starring Mabel Normand; *Out of the Fog,* starring the Great Nazimova; and *Hearts of the World,* starring the Gish sisters.

Despite the arrival of the silver screen, the years between the world wars, af-

Above: Tall Ponderosa pines and Douglas firs, were logged with axe and cross-cut saw in the early days of Kelowna's lumber industry. Gorman Brothers Lumber Limited, a family operation which began in 1951, is still in business today. More than 30 percent of the employees have been with the company more than 10 years. Courtesy, Kelowna Museum Association

Left: Kelowna soil proved very suitable for tobacco growing. Two factories were established and it looked as if tobacco might become a successful enterprise. It had great difficulty, however, breaking into the market and coping with fees and duties. Courtesy, Kelowna Museum Association

ter the visit of the Prince, were, for the most part, quiet socially.

During this time Kelownans still lived a rather isolated life and growth was still agriculturally based. The tobacco industry, which had started so well, fell into decline, and in the 1930s finally ceased. A flurry of activity had occurred with the suggestion that oil was to be found in the valley. Two oil wells were sunk, but after a number of years and very large sums of money this too petered out without producing a drop of oil. Many still think that the oil-well promotion was the biggest scam ever played on the gullible citizens of Kelowna.

Selling fruit was the most important activity for the Kelowna economy. Packing had by this time become an important part of the sale strategy. Various packs were developed, and the women and girls competed to see who could pack the best boxes of apples in the shortest length of time. Apples at that time were all individually wrapped in a square of tissue paper. The women became incredibly quick at selecting the apple wrapping and positioning it. Apple-packing contests spread throughout the province.

Soon Kelowna was able to add another credit to its fruit-processing abilities. Isobel Stillingfleet, a Kelowna girl, won the top award and was acclaimed Apple Packing Queen of the British Empire. She wrapped and packed a box of 138 first-grade apples in two minutes and 15 seconds. Each apple had to be wrapped so that the tissue formed a cushion on which it rested, and each layer arranged with stems down to prevent bruising. The finals were held in Birmingham, England, and Stillingfleet was tops among contestants.

Real development of the Orchard City came after World War II. The government of British Columbia had given consider-

able thought to the resettlement of returning servicemen. There was a need for new yet economical homes, and two building schemes created these. The "War Time" housing developments saw one- and two-storey homes built, and returning veterans were given preference. Land development schemes saw Crown land being divided into 10-acre lots for servicemen to take up at very reasonable rates.

Among the people on the Returning Veterans Rehabilitation Board was a man who was destined to become one of the most outstanding men of British Columbia. This was William Andrew Cecil Bennett. He had come to Kelowna in 1930 and started a hardware business on Bernard Avenue. He entered politics and would lead the political party of Social Credit to office from 1952 to 1972. An astute businessman of integrity and vision, Bennett would bring this vision to the Province of British Columbia.

As premier he gathered men around him who, under his guidance, brought the province into its full potential. He realized roads were the key to prosperity, and his highways ministers, among whom was Phil Galardi, got busy planning miles and miles of roads. Galardi used a small plane to take him over the terrain and quickly became known as "Flying Phil."

Premier Bennett loved Kelowna. Although he had to spend much of his time in Victoria, he maintained his home in Kelowna. This lovely house, formerly the residence of F.R.E. DeHart, is set in well-tended grounds. Each summer the premier, who genuinely liked to meet with his constituents, threw an enormous garden party. Under a huge marquee were laid tables loaded with sandwiches and cakes. Tea and coffee were served and there was lemonade for the children.

Pictured here in her dressing room just before her performance in the Kelowna Memorial Arena, Barbara Ann Scott was a sparkling personality and performer. Kelowna took her to their collective hearts in a way seldom witnessed before. Courtesy, Kelowna Museum Association

This was an opportunity for all to chat with the premier, and stroll over the immaculate lawns and admire the flower gardens. The tradition was carried on by his son William ("Bill") Bennett who became premier of the province also, thus giving Kelowna the distinction of contributing two outstanding men to the development of British Columbia. Between them the Bennetts held the office of premier for over 25 years.

The resettlement of "the boys" was one of the tasks W.A.C. Bennett took on, and in the meetings of his board are reflected the ideas and schemes to make the return go smoothly. The board analyzed how many men could be absorbed into forestry-orchards, retail, etc., and a projection as to how this could be done was outlined.

In the late 1940s when the boys returned, many did not return alone. They had married girls in Britain and Europe and a good number of these settled in Kelowna. The marriages had also produced families, which also helped to bring up the population of Kelowna. Like those early

settlers these war brides had to become adjusted to the New World; they experienced the same heartaches and longings for mother country and dear familiar faces.

The building of the Memorial Arena gave Kelowna a much-needed facility to host stars and performers, as well as sports events. Board flooring could be laid over the ice surface for such entertainment. It was with delight that the war brides greeted the suggestion that Gracie Fields, a much-loved English singer known fondly as the "Lancashire Lass," should come to Kelowna. Fields was a singer who could perform both lighthearted and semiclassical songs. Her specialty were songs like "The Biggest Aspidistra in the World," a very funny and slightly ribald number, familiar to every British resident. Gracie Fields filled the hearts of the "brides" with nostalgia. After the performance she would meet with the girls backstage.

It was also in the arena, this time on the ice surface, that Canada's darling on skates performed. Barbara Ann Scott had

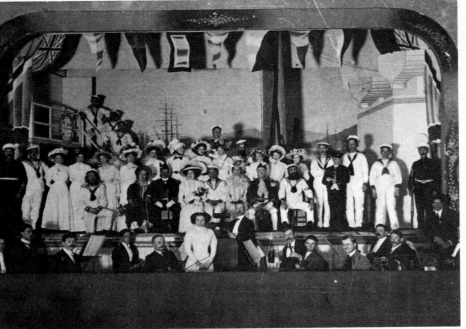

Among them (and, with such a name, a perfect choice to perform in Kelowna) was Jerry Calona, who starred in several of Bob Hope's films.

The people of Kelowna have a long tradition of performing arts. In earlier years the Okanagan Players had put on very professional shows which travelled the province. Gilbert and Sullivan light operas were popular, and the *Mikado* and *HMS Pinafore* were regular fare. At that time there were a number of Kelowna residents who had had experience on the London stage, not only in acting but also in set and costume design. The arena was not an appropriate place for staging dramatic plays, ballets, or musicals, and by now the community and church hall stages were inadequate for any ambitious production. Much thought was given to building a theatre for the performing arts. This took an enormous amount of lobbying, fundraising, and energy but in September of 1962 the new Kelowna Community Theatre was officially opened by Canadian opera star Teresa Stratas. The building was literally a barebones economy building, but it was a start.

In the early performances, little did the audience know of the sardine-like pack of actors and dancers waiting in the wings for their cues. There were no dressing rooms. All was peaceful on stage, but a regular fermentation of action was going on all around with dressers, propmen, and stagehands striving to make it all work. Somehow they did.

Although the theatre had an uphill struggle to exist at first, it has proved a tremendous asset to Kelowna. In time dressing rooms and a foyer were added. A great cross section of talent has performed in the theatre. It has also given Kelowna another tradition. Every year the Theatre Kelowna Society and the Canadian School

won the gold medal in the 1948 Olympics, and could be called the original Barbie doll, as there were dolls manufactured in her image complete with skating costume. Scott was given the Freedom of the City of Kelowna, one of a very few to be so honoured.

The arena continues to be used for headline performers. These include singer Roger Whittaker, and very recently the entrancing, spell-weaving "Zamphir."

The Kelowna Regatta had many headliners come in for the stage performances.

of Ballet have combined their talents to produce a Christmas Fantasy based on English pantomime, and a lively musical extravaganza each spring. These performances delight both young and old. International performers such as the Chinese Acrobats have "played" Kelowna.

In recent years a professional company, the Sunshine Theatre, has been formed in Kelowna. Starting with a modest run of summer presentations, Sunshine Theatre has grown into a highly professional and successful enterprise. Each year its audience grows, and so do its presentations. The company brings variety and excellence in its choice of plays, and Kelowna is treated to theatre and dramatic performances equal to many larger cities. Kelowna enjoys its theatre and plans are presently going ahead to expand the facilities.

The completion of the road to Kelowna from the coast in 1949 had been a big boost to the city's economy, but still the hold up at the lake edge was to its detriment. Something had to be done. The building of the Okanagan Lake Floating Bridge was something of a miracle. The bridge required some ingenious engineering. At first a suspension bridge seemed the answer, but the stability of the lake bottom for firm footings was suspect. So the idea of a sectioned floating bridge was developed. Once started it progressed according to plan, taking two years to build, and coming in on schedule and within budget.

Her Royal Highness Princess Margaret Rose came to officially open the bridge in 1958.

This caused a double sensation as the Princess was unmarried at the time and there had been a romance rumoured between her and a certain handsome captain, a match not encouraged by

Buckingham Palace. It was whispered that the captain had followed the Princess to the Okanagan and was staying at one of the large country houses on the lake shore. Romantic Kelowna looked upon this as a love story with the "star-crossed lovers" the victims of cruel fate. The bridge ceremonies did not exactly pale in comparison—Kelowna had looked forward to this event too long for that—but they were definitely edged out a bit when placed beside the more heart-tugging situation of a princess and a forbidden love.

On July 18, 1958, Premier W.A.C. Bennett, Mayor R.F.L. ("Dick") Parkinson, and other dignitaries escorted the Princess to the bridge. On that bright and sunny Okanagan day she picked up the gold-plated scissors and snipped the scarlet ribbon, opening the road from Kelowna to the coast.

The road, while an absolute necessity, still did not completely solve the problem of Kelowna's isolation. Any winter would see the road closed for hours, or even a day or two, when a slide blocked it. The need for alternate traffic routes was apparent. The business of getting a proper airfield had to be achieved.

Today Kelownans rely heavily on air transport, and Kelowna Airport is one of the busiest in the province. It seems hard to believe that the referendum to purchase the land for the airport passed by a single vote. It was not considered necessary—after all, planes were still considered "new-fangled."

The mayor at the time, Dick Parkinson, was a man of vision who always made Kelowna's future a top priority. He worked for years on committees, as an alderman, and as mayor to further Kelowna's options and potential. It was largely due to Parkinson that the airport became a real-

Facing page, top: Among the many Kelowna Regatta headliners was the inimitable Jerry Calona, seen here on the right at a radio interview. One of Jerry's best known talents was the ability to hold a note so long one felt like gasping for breath just listening. He was a great success at the Regatta performances. Courtesy, Kelowna Museum Association

Facing page, bottom: Gilbert and Sullivan operas were performed regularly in Kelowna. The cast for *HMS Pinafore* is seen here in 1911. Note the sets and scenery and the formally-attired musicians. The Kelowna Music and Dramatic Society prided itself on professional performances. Courtesy, Kelowna Museum Association

ity. It was a great day for him and Kelowna when on August 11, 1960, one of the hottest days on record, the federal minister of transport, George Hees, officially opened Kelowna Airport. Today Kelowna Airport handles thousands of travellers annually. Plans are under way to lengthen the runway to accommodate jumbo-jets and international flights.

By the 1960s Kelowna was a fast-growing city. Businesses and homes were being built, the school district was expanding, a library had been built and was rapidly becoming outgrown, and the museum had moved from its small location into larger premises. Prosperity was evident.

The city boundaries had been expanded and a new phenomena, the shopping mall, had appeared. The shopping mall concept did not catch on in Kelowna in the beginning. Capri Mall, opened in 1959, was a brave experiment, and it had rough going for the first few years. People did not want to drive "way out there" to shop. They were used to the stores and the people in downtown Kelowna. If they could have looked into a crystal ball they would have seen that, in spite of the inauspicious beginnings, shopping malls were the future, and the death knell to many a downtown core. Gradu-

ally people discovered they liked the parking, the shielding from the elements, and other benefits that went with mall shopping. Capri struggled along and survived, and the first was by no means the only mall to develop. Kelowna now has several very extensive malls. The largest carries on the city's fruit-growing tradition in its name "Orchard Park." It is situated a very short distance from the original mission settlement of Father Pandosy.

Downtown Kelowna is changing its image. More and more the financial houses are consolidating in the townsite, and it is the financial hub of the community. Several banks, credit unions, trust companies, and investment houses have their main offices on Bernard Avenue today. There is still a good assortment of retail shops, and these merchants are working together to present the public with a chance to shop in a different atmosphere, rather than the enclosed malls with their repeated set of chain operations. This, for the shopping public, is the best of both worlds. The malls are there with the space and controlled atmosphere, and downtown is there for those who like the more informal and different setting for browsing, enjoying the sun, admiring the architecture, and visiting the nearby municipal offices.

Simultaneous with the introduction of the first mall came an event which would influence the development of Kelowna considerably.

This was the enforced boundary extension that occurred in 1973. Up until that time the outlying regions were all independent of one another. Among these regions can be counted Rutland, Benvoulin, and Okanagan Mission plus several smaller ones. When the New Democratic Party came to power they decreed that these areas would become part of the City of Kelowna. Overnight the area and the population more than doubled, from 20,000 residents to 50,000. This created incredible problems of responsibility for the city council. Suddenly they had to assume more road maintenance, sewers, lighting, policing, and parks administration. This had to be cost-shared and phased in over a number of years by arrangement with the provincial government. This was a very different job than the one taken on by that first council in 1905.

Kelowna has come of age in no uncertain terms, and there is no question about its ability to rebound. In the past few years there has been an increase in VIP visitors. Princess Anne and later the Queen and the Duke of Edinburgh have visited. In 1987 the Commonwealth heads of estate chose Kelowna as a site for their conference.

Kelowna is definitely here to stay and to flourish.

A band was formed as early as 1897 in Kelowna. This group was called upon to play on all festive occasions, and in 1907 was given a grant of $150 by the city council. A portion of this was earmarked for the purchase of a new bass horn. Courtesy, Kelowna Museum Association

The Japanese Consul,
shown here in the
1930s (in the middle
of the front row),
posed for this picture
with colleagues out-
side of the Buddhist
Church in Kelowna.
Kelowna is the home
of many Japanese-
Canadians and enjoys
a sister-city relation-
ship with Kasagui in Ja-
pan. Courtesy,
Kelowna Museum As-
sociation

6

Destination: Kelowna

The native peoples, David Stuart, and Father Pandosy all came to Kelowna not knowing what they would find. They had no knowledge of the weather, the terrain, or where the waters were situated. Travellers of today have that information, yet even so, many are unprepared for the impact of the Okanagan and Kelowna.

On a bright Okanagan day it is easy to feel that somehow you have become part of a coloured postcard. Blue is the most descriptive colour of the area. The blue of the lake and the sky is unbelievable. But even on cloudy days Kelowna is blessed with colours of unique qualities—great billowy cushions of white that sail majestically across the sky, tinged in the evening with pale pink, edged with gold lace. The grey days leave a purple tone over the mountains, and the spring and fall light silhouettes the hills at sunset, making them black against a sky of palest apple green.

Autumn sees slashes of gold on the mountainsides where the tamaracks and aspens and cottonwoods turn yellow along the creeks and gullies. Winter trans-

forms the valley to a study in blue and white, or a grey symphony of colour. Then, in May, the Okanagan is pink and white and gold, with apple blossoms in the orchards and carpets of sunflowers on the hills.

In September not only the eyes are satisfied. A drive through the orchard areas rewards one with the tantalizing smell of the ripening apples on the heavy-laden trees, and one knows why Eve succumbed to the temptation of biting into a crisp, juicy apple.

The orchards are reminders of Kelowna's numerous changes. From unsettled wilderness, Kelowna arose and became the Orchard City. In the late 1980s Kelowna is at yet another threshold. Major changes are due within the next few years as a result of the Coquihalla Pass.

The Coquihalla Pass, opened in 1986, runs through the steep terrain of the province, providing a direct route from the Prairie Provinces to Vancouver. It passes quite close to the Okanagan, but does not enter it. A connector road from the pass leading into the valley will be built by

Right and facing page: Sailing, parasailing, water skiing, and fishing are some of the activities residents and tourists can enjoy on Okanagan Lake. Courtesy, Photo/Graphics

1991. This will cut hours off the travel time from the coast to the valley, and change the itineraries of hundreds planning weekend jaunts, family vacations, and business conventions. The impact on Kelowna will be intense.

And what do visitors find when they get here? If one is driving from the coast, the approach to Kelowna is across Okanagan Lake, spanned by the three-laned floating bridge. Keeping a watchful eye open for Ogopogo, one can admire the sailboats that are usually out on the water, especially on summer Sundays when there are regular sails from the Yacht Club near the bridge. On a windy day the sails are filled and the boats fairly dance across the water. Those same summer days will see water-skiers out in force making foamy patterns on the lake surface.

In the past few years a new item has been added to water sports on the lake: windsurfing. This *looks* easy, as an expert skims along the water. But all too frequently the rider, after giving a terrific acrobatic performance, will be dumped by the wind and water. For the less energetic and for youngsters there is the lovely "Hot Sands" beach, one of many in Kelowna which offer safe swimming.

New to the skies over Kelowna is quite a daring sport: hang-gliding. These huge kite-like devices look like brightly col-

oured pterodactyls of prehistoric times looking down for a tasty meal to scoop up.

If visitors to Kelowna arrive by plane, they will be surprised by the amount of water they see below them, in what is classified as semi-desert country. There are a number of small lakes in the hills surrounding Kelowna. A fisherman can go to a different lake every day of the week, all within an hour's distance. As the plane gets lower, passengers will note that Kelowna is still a major fruit-growing area. Neat rows of fruit trees and grape vines are laid out on the benchlands. Some of the orchards show mature trees, while others appear to be young stock (some of the dwarf varieties now being planted). If it is not winter they will also see the high arcs of sparkling water from the irrigation sprinklers, looking like handfuls of jewels being flung into the sunlight. Winter visitors will see the snow pack. If skiing is in their plans they have a choice of ski hills to visit. Big White ski resort and Last Mountain have skiing almost up until Easter. Night skiing is a feature of both.

The plane lands. As the airport is a few miles from the city, visitors are gradually introduced to the urban area. If our visitors are nature lovers, they may be interested in the large black-and-white birds with long tails. These are magpies, and, like the dark blue Stellars Jay, they are year-round residents, as are the bald and golden eagles. (A pair of goldens has lived close to the airport for a number of years despite the heavy air traffic.) Tall Ponderosa pine and Douglas fir trees are on both sides of the road leading to town. These become fewer, and visitors pass by the open fields where cattle graze as they approach the northside industrial area of Kelowna.

Kelowna as a destination during holidays has a lot to offer. For the past dec-

ade the term "Four Season Playground" has been used to describe the area, with good reason. Throughout the year there are special attractions. One of the most exciting and challenging is the Kelowna Apple Triathlon. This calls on the participants to combine their skills of swimming, bicycling, and running. In the weeks preceding the triathlon, it is not unusual to see cyclists clad in shiny close-fitting outfits, heads down, legs pumping, as they power their bicycles along back roads getting ready for the event. On the appointed day the participants plunge into the lake for a two-mile swim, to the cheers of the watching crowd. Then out of the lake and onto the bicycles, they begin their 26-mile ride. Passing check points that note their passing, the participants finally approach the run that will bring them back downtown, exhausted, but with a sense of achievement. Each year the number of participants increases, and the triathlon is becoming a major event.

In February there is Snow Fest when winter is on its way out and spring but a few weeks away. Snow Fest has something for everyone. "Snow golf" is especially fun. Teams dress up in incredible outfits—from wide-striped prisoner costumes, complete with ball and chain, to large-sized baby outfits, with lacy bonnets and bibs. It is doubtful that anyone cares about counting strokes, but a great time is had by all. Hardy fishermen also brave the elements in the annual Sno Fest Derby, to see who can catch the largest fish. There is a parade down Bernard Avenue, and popping up all over the place is Sno-Go, the friendly snowman who delights children and welcomes visitors. Each year Snow Fest makes the shortest month speed all the faster into spring.

Since the 1950s, tourism has bloomed in Kelowna, and with the visitors has come development. Yet, wisely, the city still preserves the open spaces and natural beauty those same visitors hope to find. Photo by Bill Staley

Above: These rustic log buildings on the Father Pandosy Mission embody the peculiar combination of idealism and ruggedness that characterized Pandosy himself. Photo by Jerg Kroener

Right: These metal-rimmed wagon wheels at the Father Pandosy Mission recall the many aching miles Pandosy and his men traveled. Courtesy, Photo/Graphics

The MV *Fintry Queen* waits to glide away with those hungry for a taste of nostalgia, or thirsty for a draught of the blue-on-blue of Okanagan Lake on a cloudless June day. Photo by Jerg Kroener

Right: It may look like an assembly line, but it smells like Eden in September when the Goldens ripen in the Okanagan Valley. Golden Delicious were one of only a few non-red varieties to enjoy early acceptance. Photo by Jerg Kroener

Below, far right: A relative newcomer on the apple scene, the Spartan is now becoming very popular. The variety was developed at the valley's experimental farm, specifically for local production. Photo by Bill Staley

Below, center left: Tree-ripened fruit is in a class by itself for sweetness, colour, and aroma. Visitors can even pick their own at many local orchards. Courtesy, Photo/Graphics

Below, bottom left: No less than 92 apple varieties have been grown in the Orchard City, with a select few becoming the real mainstays of the market. Early and late ripeners are important to lengthen the marketing period without producing a glut; while resistance to bruising, good colour, and shelf life are other factors in an apple's success. Courtesy, Photo/Graphics

The Orchard City has its share of vineyards as well. Kelowna's wines, made from its own locally grown grapes, have won numerous medals. Courtesy, Photo/Graphics

Experiments in grape growing have now evolved into a full-blown industry, and one can devote a whole day to visiting the valley's wineries and vineyards. Here, Cedar Creek submits some items for the browser's approval at the Cedar Creek Estate Winery Wine Shoppe. Photo by Jerg Kroener

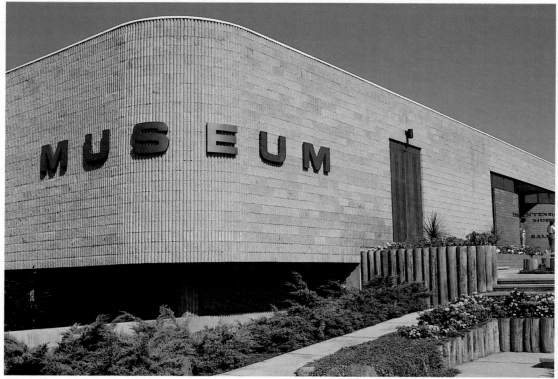

Above: The Bennett Clock stands as a monument to W.A.C. Bennett, a brilliant Kelowna businessman who went on to become a memorable premier. The supports for the clock represent the years and terms of office that her served. Courtesy, Photo/Graphics

Right: The Kelowna Museum is a National Exhibition Centre, mounting approximately eight major exhibits a year from cultures around the world. Permanent exhibits include a complete skull of a Tyrannosaurus Rex. Courtesy, Photo/Graphics

The peaceful setting of the Kasugai Gardens honors Kelowna's sister city. Courtesy, Westfile

Residents stroll through Kelowna's Citypark. Courtesy, Westfile

The billowing fluidity of a wind-filled sail is one of the simple pleasures of life in Kelowna, here immemorialized in Robert Dow Reid's *Sails* sculpture at the foot of Bernard Avenue. Courtesy, Photo/Graphics

Besides these major events there are many smaller festivities. The Rutland area has the May Queen events, and there are "blossom-time drives," special bus trips around the area which include stops for treats like scones with jam and cream, or English trifle. Canada Day sees great celebrations in the City Park with dancing and events put on by multicultural groups. In early autumn there are craft shows of all kinds, including exhibits of very fine pottery, weaving, jewelry, and paintings, all lo- cally produced. Kelowna is definitely a "Four Season Playground."

People who choose Kelowna as their permanent home can expect to have many visitors. The Okanagan sunshine, the fruit industry, the beaches, and the good shopping and dining facilities draw friends and relations like a magnet. The host and hostess are never at a loss as to where to take their visitors.

Experiments in grape growing have now evolved into a full-blown industry, so one can devote a whole day to visiting

Okanagan Lake is the site of the Annual "Frost Bite" Fishing Derby during February Snowfest celebrations. Very fine trout have been taken each year not only at derby time but all year round. Courtesy, Kelowna Museum Association

Kelowna offers some of the finest wine in the district, samples of which are seen here being tested by a Calona Wines employee. Photo by Bill Staley

the estate wineries and vineyards. Numerous medals have been won by Kelowna and district wines, which range from rich red to fine white. Calona Wines, the first of the ventures, has regular tours of its facilities. A short drive will take you to the vineyards of Cedar Creek, Mission Hill, and Gray Monk. The Gray Monk estate winery is very much a family enterprise. The whole process—from setting out and tending the vines, to harvesting and even labelling the bottles—is done by one family, who puts its trust and finances into a dream of successful grape growing and wine production.

While making the swing around the vineyards, there are many orchards one can visit also. If your visitor has a long-treasured dream of picking ripe cherries or apricots direct from the tree, there are many orchards that can gratify this desire. Tree-ripened fruit is in a class by itself. The full sugar content and colour can be enjoyed to the fullest, and wiping the juice off one's chin from a sun-warmed, ripe peach is a simple pleasure, the memory of which will last a lifetime.

If your visitors are more interested in other aspects of Kelowna, a night on the town is easy to arrange. Night clubs, both Western and disco, have some interesting entertainment, from a Dolly Parton look alike contest to local and out-of-town singers. Sunshine Theatre or Theatre Kelowna might be putting on a production, or maybe a dinner followed by a movie will fill the bill. Special interest groups abound, from stamp collecting to metal-detection clubs, and they welcome visitors with like interests. Okanagan College has so many things to offer that it's hard to choose sometimes. There are serious studies, and classes or lectures geared to leisure activities.

Pre-teens will find special delight in a visit to Bedrock City, the home of Fred Flintstone and Barney Rubble. Others will enjoy the water slide or mini-golf course next door.

Then there are people who enjoy turning back the clock and getting a glimpse of what used to be. There is a magical feeling of getting out of the "race" when one is on water. A former ferry boat, rechristened the *Fintry Queen*, makes regular trips on the lake. The world looks quite different from a boat deck. The shoreline presents all kinds of interesting views: tucked-away little coves, a small sandy beach, or a flock of water birds. Moonlight laying its path on the water casts its timeless spell, and lights reflected on calm water look like long tapering candles. After all these years, the lake—the ever-beautiful lake; the lake that, from time to time, has crested white horses whipped up by the wind; the lake that exacts a toll from those careless of its moods; the mysterious lake, with its secret caves to house who knows what monster—imparts a sense of permanence and continuity.

Another excellent way to see more of the city with little effort is to take the City Transit bus. The buses have routes that encompass all areas. Sitting high up one can look over fences at homes, old and new. Every garden has its tree, and many have several. These may be fruit trees if the house is built on ground that is a former orchard. A bus ride also takes you through the industrial side of town, where small manufacturing and warehousing takes place. Crown Forest Mill—formerly the S.M. Simpson Mill—has created a landscaped area to present a pleasing facade to passers-by. The mill, which sits behind this landscaping, is a large part of the industrial base.

The bus route goes out along Highway 97 past several shopping malls, and past the industrial park, which is home to another set of industries including Western Star Truck Company. Opened in 1967, Western Star has a 19-acre site and turns out massive trucks complete to the last detail. Throughout the ride one is reminded that the fruit industry was, is, and hopefully will continue to be a large part of the Kelowna economy. The British Columbia Tree Fruit/Sun-Rype Plant ships fruit concentrates and juices to all parts of Canada and to some 38 countries worldwide.

Arriving back downtown, one can stretch one's legs with a walk around the

A man of vision, S.M. Simpson began his own reforestation scheme to replace timber as it was logged, long before the idea of resource management existed. His one-man operation grew and was the foundation for the Crown Forest Mill. Courtesy, Kelowna Museum Association

Established in 1967 the Western Star Truck Company represents one of the major employers for the Kelowna area. Courtesy, Western Star Truck Co.

park or by visiting the city's points of interest.

The sculpture *Sails* by Robert Dow Ried stands at the foot of Bernard Avenue beside the lake shore. It is beautiful from all angles. When looking down the street, one sees it standing out against the blue waters. A tall, glistening white, tapering sculpture, its graceful lines embody the fluid, free feeling of a wind-caressed sail.

A few blocks away is another monument. The Bennett Clock stands high above its supports, arranged to represent the years and terms of office that W.A.C. Bennett served. At the foot of the clock is a cascading fall of water. Many office workers and tourists enjoy their summer brown-bag lunches sitting in the sun beside the cool water.

Just behind the Bennett Clock is a secluded and beautiful area. Step through the gates and you are in another world. Here in the heart of Kelowna is a Japanese garden, built to honour Kelowna's sister city Kasagai in Japan. Cascading water falls into a small pool where it becomes a placid area for water plants. The little waterway is spanned by a traditional Japanese bridge, and the surrounding gardens are filled with flowering shrubs and plants arranged to create a reflection of the Orient. Kasagai Gardens and Veendam Way in City Park are an ever-present reminder of Kelowna's international links with its sister cities.

In the Kelowna Museum is an item guaranteed to bring joy to every youngster that has ever learned to say the word "dinosaur." This is the huge complete skull of the king of dinosaurs, Tyranosaurus Rex, which is on permanent exhibit. Kelowna Museum is also a National Exhibition Centre, which means that approximately eight times a year a dif-

ferent major exhibit is mounted. This could be on any of a huge range of subjects— from Innuit (Eskimo) carvings, to the ceremonial masks of Papua, New Guinea. You might even get there in time for an ethnic "goodie" being served by the group whose culture is currently on display.

For the model railway buffs there is a magnificent display being built in the Laurel Packing House just down the street from the museum. This is a masterpiece of diorama construction with tunnels and trestle bridges carrying the trains over and under the complicated terrain.

The Laurel Packing House is adjacent to the area where a new waterfront development is planned. This will include a convention centre and hotel and all the auxiliary support services, to be built within the next five years. The design will complement the curved shoreline of the lakefront. This will certainly, along with the Coquihalla connection, bring much more convention traffic to Kelowna.

In the fall of 1987, the heads of the British Commonwealth of Nations convened here, and carried away memories of not only a good conference but of the blue Okanagan Lake and skies. Perhaps such a setting makes for thoughtful decisions.

Investors, too, see much potential here. Kelowna has seen the scope of trades and services expand tremendously in the past few years. New ideas have brought new industry, and recently the City of Kelowna applied to the provincial government for release of land from the Agricultural Reserve in anticipation of expansion to come.

In 1973, when the boundaries of Kelowna were expanded, there were some concerns about orderly development. Kelowna expansion was so drastic and broad that many of the ideas for the "ideal city" simply could not be financed

Bankhead Pond was the scene of many a hockey game. Spectators bundled up in heavy coats, long skirts, and woollen scarves and socks. This pond has long been filled in, but Bankhead School keeps the name and memory of the district alive. Courtesy, Kelowna Museum Association

at first. This, in a way, was fortunate, as the "off with the old and on with the new" concept could not be enacted. Urbanization was also somewhat complicated by the "green belt" system known as the Agricultural Land Reserve. The expansion took in such a wide area that agricultural land fell within city limits. This land was, and in some instances still is, considered farmland and could not be developed for other purposes.

Many of the area's heritage homes and sites, including the Pandosy Mission site, are now within city limits. The people of Kelowna realized there was considerable risk of losing these links to our past, and several groups have energetically worked to save, restore, and recycle to other uses some of our finest heritage buildings. The City of Kelowna has shown consideration and leadership in this. A City of Kelowna Heritage Advisory Committee was formed to help investigate and ad-

dress heritage concerns. The result is that today one can visit the Pandosy Mission site, and arrange a nondenominational wedding in the restored Benvoulin Church. The church has pews set in the traditional curved pattern and fine acoustics suitable for music recitals. The Laurel Packing House, Kelowna's first designated heritage building, will house western Canada's only Fruit Industry Museum, while another portion of the building provides office space for the Kelowna and District Arts Council, the Multi-Cultural Association, the Okanagan Symphony, the Kiwanis Music Festival, Sunshine Theatre, and other culturally oriented groups.

Guisachan House, the home built for the Earl and Countess of Aberdeen, is currently being restored, even down to the beautiful English garden setting. Close by is John McDougal's log house, moved to secure foundations with its logs and shake roof in top condition. A "heritage inventory" has been made, and the city knows which buildings are considered "Class A." These will be given special consideration in future development.

While an awareness of the past is here, it has in no way stunted Kelowna's development.

Between downtown and the waterfront development will sit a number of municipal and provincial buildings. It is planned to situate a new courthouse here to tie in with the expansion currently under way at the police administration buildings. Kelowna City Hall, which has just undergone extensive renovations, also sits within this administrative core, near to the Kelowna Community Theatre.

This whole area is saved from the fate of some city centres of "too much too close" by the buffering presence of Kasagai Gardens and the Bennett Clock.

The city council has made a number of studies to successfully interface cultural activities, downtown development, waterfront development, and the presence of municipal, federal, and provincial government buildings. The council will never be able to please everyone, but on the whole it has done well. People come to Kelowna, like it, and want to live here. (In fact the numbers coming in from time to time exceed the city's capacity to absorb them.) The economy is good and constantly growing. Housing is going ahead very steadily with special attention given to the needs of those coming here to retire.

It takes some clever juggling of resources to make any city all things to all people. Among the top concerns is health care. Vital to a good health-care system are hospitals and other medical services. Also important to a city are the water and sewage systems, recreational facilities, and fire protection. On the whole, Ke-

lowna gets full marks for all of these.

The Kelowna General Hospital is fully up to date and exceedingly active. It is equipped to handle practically every type of situation, while the Cottonwoods Extended Care Facility, administered by the hospital, copes with extended-care needs.

Few history books deal with sewage disposal, although it has been at the root of many health disasters. Disposal has created difficult problems as settlements have grown to towns, and towns to cities. Throwing the water out the back door sufficed in early times, but more people meant more sophisticated approaches were needed. Septic tanks were built for water disposal, and that unlovely but vital piece of equipment, the "Honey Wagon," was used to deal with more difficult waste disposal. Garbage dumps had to be established and then pickup service arranged.

In later years, as people became more aware of their environment, there arose the problem of finding an acceptable solution to sewage disposal. Discharge into the lake was acceptable when there was only a handful of people. Now it is unthinkable to discharge untreated effluent in such a way. After considerable study, city leaders decided on what they feel is the best answer to the disposal problem. They opted for the Bardenpho System, considered to be consistently reliable in the removal of undesirable chemical components from water. Kelowna started the project in 1980. It was completed in 1982, and the success can be measured by the experiment to raise rainbow trout in the processed effluent. None of the 150 fingerlings died; in fact they flourished, and there is now a similar project to raise Kokanee to restock the lake. At the same time the water system has been expanded to encompass an enormous area. Miles of wa-

The Kelowna Packers, pictured here in the Memorial Arena, were the hometown hockey team. The team worked as a splendid unit and became the Canadian amateur team chosen to go to Russia to play in amateur competition. Courtesy, Kelowna Museum Association

ter lines have been installed, and water carried in them contains flouride as a measure against tooth decay.

A concern for health has also given Kelownans a reputation as physically active. Memorial Arena is the place for hockey and skating, while the "roaring game" of curling is played in the Kelowna Curling Rink. Other activities needed different types of facilities, and as a result the Parkin-

son Recreation Centre was built. It was named for Dick Parkinson who, besides being Kelowna's long serving mayor, was an ardent sports fan, as well as a player and coach. The recreation centre includes an indoor swimming pool and space for numerous activities.

Not far from the Parkinson Recreation Centre stands the fire hall. This impressive building has no resemblance to the

H. Campbell Capt.

C. Pettman

H. Ryan

D. Poole

Kelowna Famous Players

D. Parkinson

Coach

1934

1935

B.C. Champion Sr. "B"

T. Forbes

M. Meikle

K. Griffith

G. McKay

H. Pettman

Ribelin Photo

first little fire house, big enough only to tuck in the hand pumper and hoses of early times. When that first fire house—spurred into being by the forceful words of George Rose—was outgrown in 1906, the fire brigade moved into a smart white-painted building with a tower, situated downtown. In time this one was torn down and a new brick one built on the same lot. As the fire bri-gade grew and as more equipment was ac-quired, the building grew too. In 1914, when an up-to-date ladder truck was proudly added in all its shining red glory, it was just a smidge too long to fit into the fire hall. No problem. A hole was punched in the back wall for the ladder to poke through. The red brick hall is still there and still used by the fire department.

Kelowna took to basket-ball in no uncertain terms. Dick Parkinson was both a player and a coach and led the Ke-lowna team to cham-pionship status in 1934 and again in 1935. Cour-tesy, Kelowna Museum Association

Today there are several branches of the Kelowna Fire Department. These are mostly halls that were formerly the headquarters of the volunteer fire departments serving the outlying districts. With the expansion of city boundaries, these districts became part of the city and the halls were incorporated into the Kelowna Fire Brigade System.

Fire protection in Kelowna is very efficient. Many buildings have direct alarm systems connected with the halls for instant notification. The crews have excellent training and equipment. A valuable item added in the past few years is the "jaws of life," a large mechanized device for cutting away metal to release victims in accident situations. The new main fire hall on Highway 97 near the recreation centre houses the finest of equipment.

The firemen do an enormous amount of work creating fire-prevention awareness, starting at the school level. Until very recently the ambulance service was also run from the fire hall. This valuable service was passed on from team to team over the years and was an intrinsic part of the system. It is now run as a separate unit.

* * *

As a destination for permanent residence, Kelowna has everything to offer in schools, medical care, housing, leisure time activities, and one of the continent's more bracing climates.

As a long-time Kelowna resident, this writer has developed a protective and slightly selfish attitude. Part of me says, "Come to Kelowna, I love showing it off," but the other part says, "Don't come if you want to spoil it, exploit it, and only take from it." Places like Kelowna are reminders of what is good in the world.

Development, however, is inevitable, and indeed essential. One cannot lock both ends of the valley in a futile attempt to halt change.

Besides being a destination, Kelowna has a destiny. Hopefully the city will be able to maintain the beauty and bounty of its past, and will never underestimate its restorative value. A fitting conclusion to this book is to quote, in total, a letter to the editor of the *Kelowna Record,* written in 1918:

Dear Sir:

It will of course, be of no interest to your readers to know that we have left your beautiful city—except to be sure we have gone. Two weary men let loose in a city to which they are strangers might leave weary men still. We were such men, but we leave your city not as weary men, but as cheerful refreshed men. The reason is not hard to give. It is because your city and surroundings are beautiful and inspiring; your people are hospitable and kind. To us the memory will ever be sweet and we leave knowing that you have a wonderful future. We see great prosperity ahead for your citizens and although you have trials, and will have trials, we are sure you will rise triumphant and become a contented and prosperous community.
Water is water, but to you water is your very existence, and we are sure that in this direction your difficulties will soon be overcome. We leave, to again return. In the interval we will sing the praises of Kelowna and its people.
Yours Truly,
The (2) Arthurs
A.J. Kappele
A.C. Boswell.

The predictions of the "(2) Arthurs" came to pass. Kelowna did indeed become a thriving community.

As Kelowna approached the half-century mark, it was felt that something very special should be created to mark

the event. An emblem incorporating the many facets of the city was decided upon. Kelowna's Coat of Arms, designed for the 50th Jubilee in 1955, is truly representative of Kelowna and its people.

The City of Kelowna's Armorial Bearings were officially accepted by the city council on January 3, 1955. The shield, with wavy blue lines on white at the base, depicts Okanagan Lake from which rise three white piles, representing mountains. Above these, on a blue sky, are two apples on gold. Astride the shield, knightly armour, surrounded by a wreath, supports a tree bearing apples. At the base of the tree, a crosscut saw is emblematic of the lumbering industry and the early pioneers.

The supporters are, on the dexter side, a grizzly bear, indicating the derivation of the city's name, and on the sinister side, a seahorse, which is the nearest thing in heraldry of our Ogopogo.

The motto, "Fruitful in unity," alludes to Kelowna's steady progress, largely attributable to its basic fruit industry and the community mindedness and cooperation of its citizens.

May it always be so.

This beautiful shot of the Okanagan Lake Bridge was taken on an early winter evening. Courtesy, Kelowna Museum Association

Pictured here in 1912, the Burns Meat Market was situated on Bernard Street. It reflects the butchers' trade at its best. Note the fresh sawdust on the floor, the immaculate white outfits, the elaborate meat-rack with its ornate ironwork decoration and, of course, the string holders suspended from the ceiling. Courtesy, Kelowna Museum Association

7

Partners in Progress

The partners who have joined in the presentation of *Kelowna: An Illustrated History* reflect the diversity commonly equated with the strength of this community set in the heartland of the Okanagan Valley.

Although much about the economic life of Kelowna has changed since its incorporation in 1905, the community's heritage is still clear to see from every viewpoint overlooking the city. The forests that supply the raw material for Kelowna's largest industry form a soft mat of green on the surrounding hills. Below these, orchards and vineyards blend into the residential and commercial centers of the city, providing a unique visible link between Kelowna's still-thriving agricultural heritage and the modern economic and population growth that typifies the city today. Curving in a grand sweep around the western edge of Kelowna is Okanagan Lake, which provides a central hub to the ever-growing tourist industry.

This visible display of the interconnection of Kelowna's economic life is re-flected in these pages by the mix of businesses portrayed: Some have historic roots in the Okanagan that predate Kelowna's incorporation; others played vital roles in its early formation.

Most have more recent histories. This is not a surprising fact, but merely a further reflection of Kelowna's reality. It is important to note that in 1961 the entire population of the Central Okanagan Regional District, which encompasses Kelowna, was slightly more than 27,000. In 1986 that figure had mushroomed to approximately 90,000. This continuing population growth reflects the movement of an increasing number of businesses to the community, which in turn serves to create the broader economic base capable of supporting further growth.

The businesses included in the following pages have actively supported this publication in that same spirit of community service and development. Typical of the business community's civic spirit is the Kelowna Chamber of Commerce's sponsorship of this popular history of the city in which its members live and prosper.

Kelowna Chamber of Commerce

Since its incorporation on June 13, 1906, the Kelowna Chamber of Commerce has assumed a key role in the economic, political, cultural, and social life of the community. Today, with a membership of more than 1,000, the chamber is composed of businessmen and individuals dedicated to making Kelowna an increasingly vital economic center and ensuring it retains its status as being among one of the most pleasant communities in Canada.

As longtime publisher of the *Kelowna Daily Courier* and chamber president in 1947, R.P. MacLean wrote in 1968: "The work of the chamber touches nearly every citizen."

MacLean lauded the chamber's work at tourist promotions, encouraging Kelowna's consideration as a convention site; leadership in attracting new businesses to the city; leading role in community affairs, encouraging community interest in politics, and health and safety work; and encouragement of better traffic, parking, and highway regulations.

Although written in 1968, MacLean's thumbnail sketch of the chamber's activities reflects the work still carried on. While the work is sim-

ilar, the cost required to do that work has increased tenfold. In 1968, 615 members funded a chamber budget of $43,335. Twenty years later slightly more than 1,000 members funded the $422,000 budget necessary to operate a sophisticated tourist-promotion, business-information, and government-lobbying organization.

Because of the chamber's role as a focal point in community affairs, many notable Kelowna citizens have served as chamber presidents. W.A.C. Bennett, chamber president from 1937 to 1938, was B.C.'s premier from 1952 to 1972. His son, Bill Bennett, was a chamber president in 1966, and B.C. premier from 1975 to 1985. Larry Chalmers, chamber president in 1984 was elected to the provincial legislature in 1985. Several of the city's mayors have also served as chamber presidents.

The Kelowna Chamber of Commerce has frequently been vital in anticipating the future economic directions of the community. In 1961, when the Okanagan was primarily known as an agricultural and forestry economic region, the chamber executive foresaw the vital role tourism would come to

play in the valley's life. That year tourist promotion became an integral part of the chamber's activities.

By 1963 it was apparent to the chamber executive that a growing community required a more broadly based economic structure to maintain stable development. In concert with the City of Kelowna, the chamber formed an industrial commission to attract new businesses to the city. That commission played a vital role in drawing many of the larger industrial and commercial firms that now are part of Kelowna's economic community. The Economic Development Commission continues that role today, working closely with the chamber in fostering continued growth.

The success of the Kelowna Chamber of Commerce's work since its incorporation in 1906 is evidenced by the growth of Kelowna from a small agricultural center to the economically diverse city it is today.

The Business & Economic Resource Center on Harvey Avenue is home of the Kelowna Chamber of Commerce.

Marathon Shopping Centres

The emergence of Orchard Park Regional Shopping Centre as the heart of Kelowna's prime commercial district has brought the city full circle to its historical roots. It was the very spot where the Interior's largest indoor shopping mall is today located that was first set aside in 1891 as the townsite for what would eventually become Kelowna. G.G. Mackay laid out the townsite of Benvoulin there and contracted out the completion of a small hotel, completed in 1892.

Only the introduction of sternwheeler service on Okanagan Lake a few years later prevented development of this site into the commercial hub. With the sternwheelers, a lakeside siting of the town became preferable, and the Benvoulin townsite was abandoned.

It was not until August 3, 1971, the old townsite realized Mackay's dream and became a thriving commercial concern. On that day the first phase of Orchard Park opened on a 26-acre rectangular site bordered by the city's two major conduits—Highway 97 and Springfield Road. The mall featured as its main stores a Sears, Shoppers Drug Mart, and a

branch of the Canadian Imperial Bank of Commerce.

The following summer the Hudson's Bay Company (now The Bay) joined as the second major anchoring tenant and the mall, now with about 48 stores, rapidly became known as a destination shopping point for all the Okanagan and surrounding area.

The mall was developed by Marathon Shopping Centres, a division of Marathon Realty Company Limited. Marathon Realty is a Canadian corporation that develops, owns, and manages other industrial and business developments across Canada and the United States. It is a wholly owned subsidiary of Canadian Pacific Limited, a diversified major Canadian Corporation headquartered in Toronto.

Marathon has since ensured that the mall grows apace with the increasing development of Kelowna.

After 10 years of operation, Marathon again instituted a major expansion to recognize the rapid growth of Kelowna and the Okanagan during these years. A Woolco department store and a large Safeway were added as anchors, with an additional 45 smaller outlets constructed. Further

smaller expansions were carried out in 1987, and in 1988 much of the mall was redecorated and a WoodWynn store added.

Today the mall houses 106 stores and services in 514,134 square feet of leasable space. It is the largest shopping center between Vancouver and Calgary.

This prominence has led to its recognition as a regional shopping center, serving not only Kelowna, but surrounding communities ranging from Osoyoos in the south to Salmon Arm in the north, with an estimated population base of about 250,000 people.

The development of Orchard Park in the old townsite, 2.7 miles north of downtown Kelowna, has influenced the city's commercial growth. In the vicinity of the mall are numerous other smaller commercial developments and a large industrial park. Consequently, Orchard Park has now become the commercial heart of Kelowna—just as G.G. Mackay planned back in 1891.

Standing on the site set aside in 1891 to be the town centre is Kelowna's Orchard Park Regional Shopping Centre, Marathon's largest retail development in Western Canada.

Doppelmayr Lifts Ltd.

The locating of Doppelmayr Lifts Ltd. in Kelowna came about through happenstance in 1966, but now this site is seen as a fundamental factor in the rapidly rising growth of the Canadian arm of the multimillion-dollar, privately owned, Austrian-based corporation.

In 1966 two Kelowna men, Doug Mervyn (now successful owner and operator of Alkali Lake Ranch, the oldest and one of the largest cattle ranches in British Columbia) and Cliff Serwa (elected Social Credit Member of the Legislative Assembly for the Okanagan South Riding in November 1986), were looking for a ski lift for their infant Big White Ski Resort, under construction in the excellent powder snow mountains east of Kelowna. Their search took them to Wolfurt, Austria, where Konrad Doppelmayr had pioneered many advances in the ski lift industry after founding the company in 1892.

Serwa and Mervyn left Wolfurt so

impressed with Doppelmayr's lift technology that they came away not only with a T-bar lift for Big White, but also the rights to begin marketing Doppelmayr lifts in western North America. For the first few years the Kelowna arm of Doppelmayr operated out of a small office on Water Street in the downtown area. In 1970 the company moved to a larger, chalet-shape facility surrounded by forest on Hall Road in the lower end of East Kelowna's orchard country. It remains

Neither helicopters nor cranes, but pure manpower was responsible for the installation of a Doppelmayr triple chairlift in Pakistan in 1987.

there today.

In the same year as Doppelmayr in Kelowna was being moved, its future president, Georg Schurian, was beginning work for the Austrian parent corporation as a lift installer. Over the next six years he gained experience in installing ski lifts on the ground and by helicopter on mountains throughout Austria, and literally learned about the lift industry from the ground up.

During this time Schurian met Mervyn's daughter, Rhonda, on a skiing trip in Europe. When he came to Kelowna in 1976 to visit Rhonda, Schurian ended up staying to marry her and began working for Doppelmayr in Kelowna as an installer.

In 1978 Mervyn sold his share in Doppelmayr and Schurian bought in. Shortly thereafter, Cliff Serwa, Glen Mervyn, John West, and Peter Van Vreumingen also ceased to be shareholders. Five years later Schurian had worked his way up through the ranks to become the president of the Kelowna arm of Doppelmayr.

During these years the marketing ef-

Doppelmayr's gondolas, like this one operating at Lake Tahoe, are designed to carry from six to 24 passengers.

forts of the Kelowna operation were creating sales of lifts from South Dakota to Saskatchewan to Alaska. The company established a reputation for reliability of construction, meeting deadlines and providing strong after-sale support and maintenance.

Doppelmayr now has roughly 350 ski lifts installed on mountains throughout Canada. They range in value from $100,000 T-bars to major gondola lifts selling for $20 million. The proliferation of Doppelmayr lifts has resulted in the corporation capturing some 75 percent of the western Canadian market. A major achievement was the construction of all lifts used on Mount Allan, near Calgary, for the alpine events of the 1988 Winter Olympics.

The Kelowna office has a permanent staff of 10, including a professional engineer, gear box expert, parts manager, accountant, and service personnel; together it orchestrates networks of supervisors and crews in the field across Western Canada and the United States. Ski lift construction is a seasonal industry, and during the summer construction season, staff working out of Kelowna grows to approximately 70 people.

All spare parts and servicing of the lifts in Western Canada come from Kelowna, and Doppelmayr draws heavily upon the community for what materials can be produced locally rather than in Austria or at Doppelmayr's manufacturing plant in the Montreal suburb of St. Jerome, Quebec. The St. Jerome manufacturing plant, employing 100 people, produces two-thirds of the equipment needed for lifts constructed in North America now, and its size will double by 1990. This expansion will allow more lift parts to be constructed in Canada, avoiding the added cost of importation from European plants.

The growth of Doppelmayr's Eastern Canada operation corresponds with growth of the Kelowna arm. A move is planned for the company to relocate to a new, larger facility on Highway 97 near the Kelowna Airport. The new building will have enlarged office and warehouse space and room for future growth.

Schurian foresees a long-range possibility of more of the manufacturing aspect of lift construction coming to Kelowna. Already several million dollars are spent in the community annually through equipment purchases and subcontract work.

The locating of Doppelmayr's Western Canadian operation in Kelowna, Schurian says, was total happenstance. But the company has stayed on in the city "because of the geographically excellent nature of the location. It is right in the middle of the ski resorts of western North America. If you draw a circle on the map with Kelowna as the center you are equidistant to most of the major mountain ranges where the ski resorts are situated."

This advantageous location allows Schurian and his support staff to be able to fly into ski resorts on the coastal mountains or in the midst of the Rockies with equal ease—a factor that gives Doppelmayr a significant edge in bidding for lift construction and maintenance contracts. "There is a lot of competition in the lift construction field," Schurian says, "and it is the quality and type of product we offer operators, combined with our unique ability to provide service, that help us keep the level of business we have."

Above: The very latest in lift technology is demonstrated by Doppelmayr's four-seater, detachable Bubble Chair, installed at Blackcomb, British Columbia; Mt. St. Anne, Quebec; and Vail, Colorado.

Right: Detachable quad chairlift at Blackcomb, British Columbia.

Western Bus Lines of B.C. Ltd.

The expanding importance of the transportation industry is well evidenced in the growth and diversification marking the development of Western Bus Lines of B.C. Ltd.

Ray Therrien, the current owner and president, started his charter bus operation in October 1974, when he purchased the two older coaches operated by the Penticton-based Impala Coach Lines, started by Mickey Schreader and Don Norse 10 years earlier. At the time a new coach cost approximately $72,000.

By 1976 Therrien needed to expand. He acquired more buses by purchasing Western Bus Lines of B.C., then based in Kamloops.

Therrien operated the bus line under this name until 1978, when he sold the charter bus business to David Jensen of the Kelowna suburb of Winfield. From 1978 to 1980 Therrien owned only one coach, operated under the name of Fareway Bus Lines. He also owned and managed Galaxy Coach, Sales, Service & Leasing in Penticton—a bus servicing, sales, and leasing business.

In 1980 Therrien bought back Western Bus Lines of B.C. Ltd. and combined its bus charter operation with Fareway Bus Lines. Since then Western Bus Lines has been expanded to its current usual complement of roughly 10 Highway coaches.

Western Bus Lines leases its coaches to tour companies, schools, sports organizations, and numerous other clients. The firm's coaches are licensed to travel anywhere in North America, and Western Bus Lines holds pick-up rights from Kamloops south on Highway 97 to the U.S.-Canadian border. Since opening an auxiliary office in Vancouver in 1986, Western Bus Lines has expanded its pickup rights to include the Vancouver area.

Throughout most of its recent history, Western Bus Lines has had an average complement of some 12 employees, mostly drivers. Mechanic Ted Sylvester, who has been with the company for more than 12 years, maintains the buses at the Penticton shop facility, operated under Galaxy Coach Sales, Service & Leasing. Administrator Zinnia Lang, a seven-year employee, works out of the Kelowna Western Bus Lines office, which is shared with Sunwest Tours Ltd. All of Sunwest Tours' various tourist travel packages entail the leasing of Western Bus Lines' coaches.

In 1988 Western Bus Lines expanded the quality of its transportation service with the addition of four Canadian-made Prevost coaches worth $250,000 each. The Prevost coach is considered one of the most luxurious and reliable in the industry.

Currently Western Bus Lines of B.C. Ltd. has applied to operate daily deluxe individual passenger fares from the interior to Vancouver and back. It is this kind of commitment to continually improve services that has made Western Bus Lines a leader in Kelowna and British Columbia transportation.

Western Bus Lines' luxurious new Prevost coach, a recent addition to the fleet, ensures a comfortable ride for the traveller.

Levin, Kendall & Company

The law firm of Levin, Kendall & Company had its roots in a one-man firm set up by Samuel Casey Wood, born in Toronto in 1940. Wood graduated from Osgoode Hall Law School in 1964 and soon after sailed for Africa, meeting his wife to be, Jane, on the ship. They lived in Rhodesia for a short time and after returning to Canada decided to come to Kelowna in 1970, partly because the countryside reminded them of Rhodesia.

Wood started the first law practice in the Rutland area in 1971, situated in the Canadian Imperial Bank of Commerce building on Park Road. Two years later he was joined by William J. Thiessen, and the firm moved to 143 Park Road.

In 1977 Casey Wood died suddenly, and shortly thereafter the firm was purchased by Duncan A. Brown and William Tymchuk, who were later joined by Joseph T. Hattori.

These three partners operated the practice until 1982, when they were joined by Robert O. Levin (LL.B., University of Manitoba). Thomas G. Kendall (LL.B., University of British Columbia) subsequently joined the firm and in 1984 it was renamed Levin, Kendall & Company.

The firm now consists of four partners, Levin, Kendall, Sandra G. Kochan, and Christopher R. Penty, and associate John Lauinger.

Levin's practice is now restricted to civil litigation. He was first called to the Bar in Manitoba in 1974 and moved to Kelowna six years later. He has been active in several capacities at the Big White Ski Resort area since

Serving Kelowna's legal needs are Levin, Kendall & Company partners (from left): Christopher R. Penty, Sandra G. Kochan, Thomas G. Kendall, and Robert O. Levin.

his arrival, and has served as chairman and board member of the Central Okanagan Child Care Resources Society and as executive member and past president of the Okanagan Jewish Community Association.

Kendall has practiced in British Columbia since 1960 and specializes in corporations and businesses engaged in industrial or commercial ventures. For most of his adult life, Kendall has bred and raced thoroughbred horses. He continues a "backyard" breeding operation from his farm in Oyama, British Columbia.

The community has been well

served by Kendall, whose community involvement includes being president elect of the Rotary Club of Kelowna-Rutland, and a member of such organizations as the Economic Development Committee, Estate Planning Council, Rutland Citizens Patrol, Rutland Community Society, the Planned Giving Committee of Kelowna General Hospital, and the Kelowna Chamber of Commerce.

Since joining the firm in 1983 Sandra Kochan (LL.B, 1980, University of Saskatchewan) has practiced general law, including corporate and commercial work, conveyancing, family law, general civil litigation, wills, estates, and administrative law. She and her husband reside in neighboring Peachland, where her family and husband own and operate an estate winery. She is secretary of the Kelowna Film Society, past board member of the Central Okanagan Emergency Shelter Society, executive member of the Kelowna Bar Association, and a member of the Sierra Club, the Kelowna Folk Club, and the Kelowna Women's Resource Center.

Kelowna native Christopher Penty (LL.B., 1982, University of Victoria) joined the firm in 1985, became a partner two years later, and is involved in general practice. He is the only member of the firm to practice criminal law and serves as vice-president of the Kelowna Bar Association.

Levin, Kendall & Company employs six full-time staff and two part-time staff. The firm serves clients throughout British Columbia, but most are from the Okanagan Valley region.

Fletcher Challenge Canada Ltd.

The Simpson Timber Mill at Manhattan Beach, circa 1935.

As Kelowna's single-largest employer, Fletcher Challenge Canada Ltd. emphasizes the historic prominence of the forest industry in the city's economic life. Stands of Lodgepole Pine, Englemann Spruce, and Douglas Fir found on the mountain ranges surrounding the Okanagan Valley are a rich source of timber, and since the early years of Kelowna's founding lumber companies have grown by harvesting the forest.

Fletcher Challenge Canada's roots in Kelowna can be traced back to 1913, when Stanley M. Simpson started a small sawmill next to what is now the downtown fire department on Water Street. The small mill specialized in sash and door construction with a staff of roughly 12 people.

Simpson moved his operation into the empty Kelowna Cannery Company building at the intersection of Ab-

bott Street and Leon Avenue in 1918. By 1924 the mill had grown to such a size that he incorporated as S.M. Simpson Ltd. and branched out into a new growth industry—manufacturing container boxes for the burgeoning Okanagan fruit industry.

The company's staff in 1924 grew to some 50 employees as Simpson acquired controlling interest in a second mill in the Ellison area, near what is now the Kelowna Airport.

By 1931 S.M. Simpson was booming, and the firm built a veneer manufacturing plant at the Manhattan Beach location, where the Fletcher Challenge Canada mill stands today. Between 1931 and 1965, when Crown Zellerbach Canada Ltd. acquired the company, S.M. Simpson grew into the largest privately owned business in British Columbia's interior, directly em-

ploying 600 people.

From 1935 to 1965 S.M. Simpson's son, Horace Simpson, was closely involved in the firm's operation, becoming president in 1955 after his father suffered a stroke. Horace Simpson became general manager of the new Crown Zellerbach division, and later assumed a key planning role within the major Canadian lumber company.

The Crown Zellerbach operation continued to expand successful production and marketing strategies S.M. Simpson had developed. Throughout the 1960s a key product was the plywood bulk bins used by the fruit and vegetable industries to harvest and store crops.

In 1969 Crown Zellerbach announced its intention to expand the Kelowna operation to include a corrugated container plant, operated by Crown Zellerbach's Paper Products Division. The new plant, Crown's second in British Columbia, was built to serve the Okanagan Valley's growing agricultural and industrial markets. Construction of the $4.5-million plant began in August 1969. The 130,000-square-foot facility opened on Enterprise Way in September 1970 with a complement of approximately 40 hourly people and 10 management staff.

Since opening, the plant's personnel complement has risen to an average hourly work force of 60 and a management staff of 14. The majority of the paper supplies for the corrugated containers are shipped to the plant from the Crown-owned pulp mill at Campbell River with the balance purchased from other British Columbia, Washington, and Oregon pulp mills.

Today the plant's main business is still from valley industry. About one-third of the corrugated containers manufactured at the plant are used to supply the needs of the Okanagan fruit industry; Consumers Glass, Hiram Walker & Sons Okanagan Distillery, numerous valley wineries, and other businesses in the valley utilize another third. The remaining one-third is sold to businesses in Vancouver and throughout Alberta.

In 1987 the corrugated container plant underwent a $3.75-million modernization that included the installation of a new $2.5-million Martin Flexo Folder-Gluer that is fully automated and capable of four-color processing. The modernization also saw the addition of 20,000 square feet of warehouse space.

Today the lumber and plywood mill occupies 19 acres of land at Manhattan Beach, and is among the largest employers in greater Kelowna.

From the 1970 opening of the corrugated container plant to the acquisition of majority control of Crown Zellerbach by New Zealand-based Fletcher Challenge Ltd. in 1983, the Kelowna lumber and plywood operations remained the single-largest employer in the city.

In 1983, with the Fletcher Challenge purchase, Crown Zellerbach was renamed Crown Forest Industries Limited; the Kelowna lumber and plywood mills, and the corrugated plant remained key elements in the new company's operations.

The current lumber and plywood mills occupy 19 acres of land in the Manhattan Beach area, employing 400 direct employees and 150 contract loggers. Production outputs are large, with 100 million square feet of plywood, based on a three-eighths-inch thickness, coming off the line annually. In addition, the lumber mill manufactures 120 million board feet of lumber per year.

Throughout 1987 and 1988 the company carried out a major, $10-million modernization of its Kelowna mills to ensure retention of its competitive edge.

Reforestation of logged areas, using both natural and tree-planting techniques, is a major commitment undertaken by the company, which manages 1,650 square kilometres of forest within the Okanagan Timber Supply Area.

On September 4, 1988, the firm again received its present name as B.C. Forest Products, Crown Forest merged their upper-level management, and the two companies began operating as Fletcher Challenge Canada Ltd. Fletcher Canada owns 100 percent of Crown Forest and 69 percent of B.C. Forest Products.

As Crown Forest has a major operating presence in the southern Okanagan, the merger ensures that Fletcher Challenge Canada Ltd. will continue to play the same major role within Kelowna's economy that was played by its ancestors when the city's foundations were first being built.

British Columbia Telephone Company

British Columbia's telecommunications giant plays a vital role in the economic life of Kelowna—both in the operation of its Columbia area headquarters, and the essential communications services it provides to the maintenance of the strong, competitive economic activities of the community's other businesses.

Reliance on telecommunications has grown vastly since the days when B.C. Tel's predecessor in the Okanagan Valley, the Okanagan Telephone Company, was incorporated by an Act of Parliament on April 25, 1907.

Okanagan Telephone Company began operations with total working capital of $50,000 to construct, equip, maintain, and operate a telephone system throughout British Columbia's County of Yale, which stretched from the Kamloops region north of the Okanagan Valley, south through the valley to the U.S.-Canada border.

At the time only a handful of small, rural telephone lines, such as the one between the Wood home and Posthill Ranch, existed. One or two of these connected with a line installed two years earlier by the Dominion Telephone Company between

Okanagan. In 1912 Okanagan Telephone Company extended its service to Kelowna with the purchase of a small telephone line firm owned by H.H. Millie. That same year Okanagan Telephone erected a line connecting the entire Okanagan Valley.

Kelowna, located at the valley center, was an integral part of the Okanagan Telephone Company system; but it was not clear during the early history of valley telephone service that Kelowna would come to be the telecommunications center of the region.

By 1934 long-distance calls to most points of Canada became feasi-

Only three short years earlier an amalgamation of three Lower Mainland telephone companies resulted in the creation on July 5, 1904, of the British Columbia Telephone Company, Limited. But it was several decades before B.C. Tel established its presence in the Okanagan.

Indeed, in 1891, when the first telephone line built in the interior of British Columbia was strung over a five-mile distance between Posthill Ranch and the home of Thomas Wood, just north of Kelowna, there was no formal telephone company in the interior of the province.

Above left: In 1928 British Columbia Telephone Company repairmen drove Ford cars like this one.

Above right: A telephone lineman strings wire from a cart near New Denver in the west Kootenay region of British Columbia in 1916.

Vernon and Kelowna.

It was not until Okanagan Telephone Company began installing telephone systems to several communities in the northern section of the valley that telephones began to become more common throughout the

ble when B.C. Telephone Company linked its long-distance lines with Okanagan Telephone Company's at Penticton, Vernon, Salmon Arm, and Revelstoke. In 1947 Sterling Ross, one of Canada's most competent telephone engineers, studied the valley's telephone system and recommended installation of automatic dial equipment to replace the old crank system.

This modernization took a number of years, and Kelowna was converted to dial phones on April 12, 1952. By 1959 the Kelowna area's expanding population justified the addition of two sub-offices—in Okanagan Mission and Rutland—to augment the downtown office.

As of 1963 the number of telephones in the Okanagan had grown to 31,543 from only 3,200 in 1923. Okanagan Telephone Company was now an important element in the provincial telephone system, and consequently also faced financial requirements beyond the economic resources of the Okanagan. This factor contributed to the purchase in December 1966 of 97.6 percent of the firm's common shares by British Columbia Telephone Company. Okanagan Telephone Company was restruc-

gradual phasing in of this plan was undertaken.

In 1982 a wide-ranging corporate reorganization divided provincial telephone operations into five areas, with Kelowna becoming the headquarters for the large Columbia area region. This region extends from Boston Bar at the end of the Fraser Canyon, north to Blue River, east to the Alberta border, and south to the Canada-U.S. border.

By the fall of 1985 the reorganization was concluded with the completion of a new 57,000-square-foot, three-storey, $4.3-million building. The

services centers.

Kelowna is now a center pin of one of B.C. Tel's largest and most extensive operating areas. In 1987 (the latest figures available) B.C. Tel employed 568 people in Kelowna, meaning that more than one-third of all the Columbia area's 1,442 employees were based in the city. The payroll issued to Kelowna B.C. Tel employees for year-end 1987 totalled $20.4 million.

And it is inevitable, as the telecommunications world of the Okanagan has grown to embrace such innovations as autotel phone systems and ex-

tured as a subsidiary. By 1976 the number of B.C. Tel-controlled shares rose to 99.9 percent.

On December 31, 1978, Okanagan Telephone Company was merged with B.C. Tel, and all operations in the Kelowna area were henceforth carried out under the parent company's banner. At the time of the merger B.C. Tel's Columbia-area headquarters was located in Kamloops and Okanagan Telephone was based in Vernon. With the merger the decision was made to combine the two headquarters operations into one facility based in Kelowna, and a

Above left: The work crew of Vernon and Nelson Telephone Company.

Above right: Industrial Park in Kelowna is the new headquarters for British Columbia Telephone's Columbia area operations.

structure contains the Columbia area headquarters and planning personnel offices. It was constructed in the Kelowna Industrial Park adjacent to B.C. Tel's Dilworth Center facility, which was built in 1979 and houses one of the Columbia area's two switching facilities and operator

tended data communications services, that B.C. Tel's presence in Kelowna will continue to grow. This presence makes itself felt in many positive ways, such as the 1987 involvement of B.C. Tel in implementing a 911 emergency service for Kelowna and the Central Okanagan Regional District, which provides one instant number for contacting fire, police, and ambulance services. Such instantaneous service reflects the sophistication attained by telecommunications since those days in 1891, when the first telephone line linked Posthill Ranch to Thomas Wood's home.

Cedar Creek Estate Winery

When Ross Fitzpatrick bought a Kelowna estate winery in November 1986, the move represented a homecoming. Fitzpatrick had been born in Kelowna. His grandparents, Peter and Susan Fitzpatrick, bought a farm in the Belgo area in 1913. His mother's parents settled in Kelowna in 1921. For many years his father, Bud Fitzpatrick, managed fruit packing houses in the Belgo and East Kelowna areas before moving the family to the south Okanagan.

After Ross Fitzpatrick graduated from Southern Okanagan High School he completed a business administration degree at the University of British Columbia and then worked on the McPhee Royal Commission in the British Columbia fruit industry. He subse-

quently worked at both grower-owned sister companies, Sun-Rype Products Ltd. and B.C. Tree Fruits Ltd.

As a consequence of this personal and family background, Fitzpatrick always felt a special kinship with the Okanagan Valley. He planned some day to buy an orchard and return.

Between his departure from the Okanagan and his return, Fitzpatrick took postgraduate studies at the University of Maryland and the Columbia University Graduate School of Business, served as executive assistant to long-time cabinet minister Jack Nicholson in the Liberal Party's Lester Pearson government, and owned four highly successful businesses. For 10 years he owned an aircraft parts business

based in Seattle, Washington. In 1979, three years before he sold the parts company, he set up an oil and gas business in Vancouver, Westmount Resources Ltd., which he sold in September 1985. From there he acquired Viceroy Resource Corporation, a gold mining company also headquartered in Vancouver.

Among Viceroy's present activities is the development of a large open-pit gold mine in the Castle Mountains straddling the California-Nevada border, which will be the third-largest

Cedar Creek Estate Winery, nestled in the heart of a 35-acre vineyard overlooking Lake Okanagan, boasts a moderate climate and rich soil—two necessary elements for the production of premium quality grapes.

gold mine in California in 1987. Fitzpatrick also acquired controlling interest in PanAtlas Energy Inc., an oil company based in Calgary.

In the mid-1980s he began actively scouting for an Okanagan property. Fitzpatrick was 53 years old when he found what he wanted, but it was a bit more than he had anticipated.

Fitzpatrick learned that Uniacke Estate Winery was for sale. He paid $925,000 for the winery and quickly invested about another $575,000 in new wine-making equipment, expansion of the building facilities by 4,000 square feet to 6,000 square feet, and land improvements. Total investment by 1988 was $1.5 million.

Most of the expenditures enhanced the production capability and quality of the Cedar Creek Estate Winery, renamed for a stream running through the property.

To ensure high quality, Fitzpatrick acquired the services of Helmut Dotti, a 29-year veteran master wine maker who had trained at the wine-making school at Klosterneuburg, Austria. Dotti's expertise was evident

with the first exclusively Cedar Creek wines, bottled after the 1987 grape crush.

At the 1988 Intervin Wine Festival held in Toronto, Ontario, more than 1,500 wines from around the world competed for medals of honor. Only 27 medals were awarded for 1987 vintage. Cedar Creek Estate Winery—the only British Columbia estate winery to win awards—won two of the 23 bronze medals with its Johannisberg Riesling and Proprietor's Blush. At the Pacific National Exhibition 1988 Wine Competition held in August, nine of the 10 Cedar Creek wines entered won awards.

The focus on superior quality wine has created a wine tradition overnight for Cedar Creek. Well-known Vancouver wine critic John Schreiner wrote in 1988 that Cedar Creek was "the most improved winery in British Columbia." And wine writer Jurgen Gothe said in an article in the Victoria *Times-Colonist* that a wine legend was about to be created in British Columbia by Cedar Creek.

Cedar Creek wines are recognized for being dryer and slightly more sophis-

ticated than other wines traditionally produced in the Okanagan. Some of this quality is made possible by the state-of-the-art wine-making equipment Fitzpatrick has installed, which rivals the best of the small North American wineries. This includes the capability to age 2,000 gallons of white and red wine in French Limousin and Nevers oak barrels, something no other Okanagan winery is equipped for.

Twinned to the improved wine quality is an increased production level. Before 1986 the winery was producing only about one-quarter of the 30,000-gallon, or 15,000-case, production limit allowed estate wineries under British Columbia law. Provincial regulations also require all estate wines to be produced from British Columbia-grown grapes, mostly from their own vineyards, which in Cedar Creek's case cover 35 acres and are mostly vinifera.

With the 1988 crush Cedar Creek reached its maximum limit. Sales in 1988 were about 11,000 cases, and sales in subsequent years are expected to reach the entire allowed production of 15,000 cases.

Fitzpatrick finds he is spending increasingly more time at the winery. He is not a hands-off type of winery owner. What was to have been a hobby farm has become a solid business, and he uses his business experience to enhance its operation.

Cedar Creek Estate Winery is the beginning of a tradition of fine wine, Fitzpatrick says, and because his name is signed on the bottom of each bottle, the winery's proprietor is determined to ensure that excellence is always maintained and nurtured.

Face Saver Beauty Therapy, Incorporated

Djubaidah Irwin's business has paralleled the rising desire for self-expression that has typified women in the 1980s. As the owner-operator of Face Saver Beauty Therapy, Incorporated, Djubaidah has seen women come to perceive esthetics as a way of increasing their own self-identity, rather than transforming themselves into a reflective image of the latest fashion trend.

"What has become evident," she says, "is that women feel much freer

is now Zimbabwe, to one of the first white immigrant families in that country. Her childhood and adolescent years taught her an independence of spirit that dramatically influenced her life.

In the early 1960s she adopted her name Djubaidah, which in Java is a prayer for help in life's difficulties. In 1975, at age 50, she took her first cosmetology training in Vancouver and established an esthetics business with some friends. Later she and her hus-

old girls to women in their late eighties. And they come from all walks of life and income levels. What brings many of her clients is the peaceful atmosphere and the knowledge that, for the time they are there, they will have her total attention. When she is with a client, Djubaidah prefers not to break her concentration to answer the phone or serve people coming in from the street.

This dedication to her clients obviously has attracted a loyal follow-

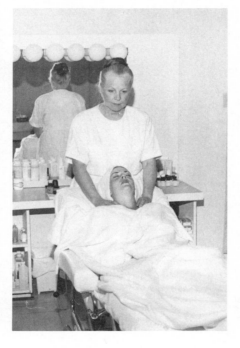

accepting themselves as they are. They are saying to themselves more often, 'I'm important. I like myself, so I am going to bring out what's best in me.'"

And often included in that desire for client self-expression are the services of private consultation, personalized aromatics, and massage offered by Face Saver Beauty Therapy.

Djubaidah understands the need for self-expression because it has been an integral part of her life for many years. She was born in 1924, in what

band moved to Kelowna and purchased an orchard, which they ran together for several years, but in 1981 she opened Face Saver Beauty Therapy in a small upstairs space on Tutt Street. The business was moved to 554 West Avenue in 1983.

Djubaidah quickly established a loyal clientele in Kelowna because of her caring service and reasonable fees. "My first love is trying to be helpful," she says. "What I do is done to the best of my ability."

Her clientele ranges from 12-year-

ing. To meet the demand, Djubaidah usually works a five-day week, starting at 6:40 a.m. and running through routinely to 6:30 p.m.

Djubaidah says this kind of regimen would not be possible without her husband's support. She adds that her entire esthetics career is proof that women have the ability to do whatever they set their minds to achieving. "So many women feel they can't be successful at starting a new business after age 50, but I have, and it has been extremely rewarding."

The Daily Courier

The history of *The Daily Courier* has paralleled the history of Kelowna. When founder R.H. Spedding arrived in Kelowna in June 1904 and established a stationery store, he recognized the need for a newspaper in the still-unincorporated community.

By July 28, 1904, Spedding had published the first issue of *The Kelowna Clarion.* Ten months later Kelowna became an incorporated community.

In those early days *The Kelowna Clarion* was published with only three staff members. Spedding acted as publisher; his son, Harry Spedding, operated the mechanical department; and W.J. Clement was both the first editor and the reporter.

On October 26, 1905, Spedding sold the business to George C. Rose, who renamed it *The Kelowna Courier and Okanagan Orchardist.* In December 1908 Rose moved the paper to a building at the corner of Lawrence Avenue and Water Street, which still stands today.

Advancing newspaper-printing technology resulted in rapid improve-

In 1976 *The Daily Courier* relocated to its present headquarters, a modern facility on Doyle Avenue.

ments. In 1909 the paper carried its first picture, and five years later a Linotype replaced the original crude typesetter.

Throughout the 1920s the paper prospered, and the building was expanded on two occasions to house the growth. In 1935, during the height of the Great Depression, the business was formed into a company, The Kelowna Courier Limited, with Rose and Donald A. Fraser retaining minority interests.

February 1938 marked the beginning of the 38-year era of R.P. MacLean at *The Courier,* when he bought an interest in the paper and replaced Rose as editor and publisher. In 1941 Rose and Fraser sold the remaining company stock to MacLean.

As the war began in 1939, MacLean simplified the name to *The Kelowna Courier* and installed new

In 1908 *The Kelowna Courier* moved into this building at Lawrence Avenue and Water Street, which still stands today. Photo circa 1928

presses. Growth slowed during the war years, so it was not until October 1946 that *The Courier* ceased being a weekly and began publishing Monday and Thursday of each week.

The year 1957 saw *The Courier* moved to a new building at Doyle Avenue and Ellis Street. The Kelowna Courier Limited was sold June 16, 1961, to Thomson Newspapers Ltd.

Advances in technological improvements continued at the paper, and circulation rose sharply during the 1960s. On February 2, 1973, installation of a Goss Community press offset system made *The Courier* one of the most modern operations in Canada.

By September 1, 1974, *The Courier* completed another move to one block up from the old building to 550 Doyle Avenue. Two years later R.P. MacLean retired and was replaced by D.F. Doucette, who remains publisher today.

Since then the presses have undergone further expansion and computerization, and the circulation has grown from 10,000 in 1976 to 17,000 in 1988.

The Daily Courier currently employs about 60 full-time staff, 25 part-time staff, 14 contract paper-delivery personnel, and more than 500 paper carriers. But the dedication to bringing Kelowna residents the news remains the same as it did when three men worked to put out that first issue.

Siesta Motor Inn

When William Saufferer first passed through Kelowna as a tourist from Western Germany in 1976, it reminded him of Lake Constance in his native country. It was then that his desire to start a new life in Canada was born.

It took a few years of planning and of finding the right business opportunity; but finally in 1980 Saufferer, then 35, purchased the 27-unit Siesta Motel on Lakeshore Road, leased out the general store his family had operated in Albershausen for 50 years, and moved to Kelowna.

The Siesta Motel had been built in 1969 by Steve Mandl, but the 11 years had not been kind to the development, and Saufferer found himself the owner of a motel in decline. He set out to turn the operation around and make it into one of the nicest motels in this tourist city. "I wanted to identify myself with the Siesta and create something nice," he remembers.

For three years the Saufferers worked hard to bring the motel back up to a sufficient level of quality. By 1983 they were ready to undertake an expansion of the motel, adding 20 more units, modernizing the older suites, and installing an indoor Jacuzzi.

The expansion was successful, and in 1985 another 18 units were added. The Siesta Motel was now U-shaped, with a large outdoor pool, courtyard, and paved parking area. With 67 units it was also about as large as the property would permit, and Saufferer thought he was through with expansions.

Such was not to be the case, however, as the adjacent property, containing only a dilapidated house, became available for sale in December 1987. Saufferer, who had always been hampered by a lack of neighboring land to expand his store in West Germany, grabbed the opportunity.

As it was difficult to integrate the new land with the Siesta Motel's structure, Saufferer elected to build a 30-unit facility called the Siesta Motor Inn and connect the two operations with corridors and a central office. The new units, opened in the summer of 1988, are one-bedroom luxury suites with private balconies. A larger indoor pool, Jacuzzi, sauna, and exercise room front onto Lakeshore Road.

Saufferer's motel operations in Kelowna have enjoyed a good reputation with tourists from around the world, he says, because of his guiding principles of management. "We treat our guests as we would want to be treated if we were travelling. You must be honest, sincere, and hardworking in this business. We spend a lot of time talking to our guests and getting to know them, and most return here year after year because of that personal relationship we have with them."

The luxury 30-unit Siesta Motor Inn and its sister facility, the 67-unit Siesta Motel, are realizations of William Saufferer's desire to create a harmonious blend of accommodation services for Kelowna visitors.

ILLUSTRATION / THE ARTS ALIVE

Hiram Walker-Allied Vintners (Canada) Limited

When the company management of Hiram Walker & Sons Limited decided in the late 1960s to establish a distillery in Western Canada, the Winfield area on the northern boundaries of Kelowna quickly became the favored choice.

The location met all requirements—transportation ease, proximity to the cool, pure water of Okanagan Lake, and 210 acres of developable land. Work on the distillery got under way in September 1969, and distillery production began in August 1971. The construction project cost more than $30 million, and further additions have added another $10 million to the value of the distillery.

Since opening, the distillery has produced whisky, vodka, gin, brandy, rum, and liqueur blends for Hiram Walker's own line of products, and it has blended and bottled products for its subsidiary companies, such as Corby's, Lamb's, Barclay's, and Wiser's.

The market areas served from the Okanagan Distillery include British Columbia, Alberta, Saskatchewan, Manitoba, Yukon, Northwest Territories, the western United States, and the Far East. Its production capacity is 7.5-proof gallons (or 19.5 million litres of absolute alcohol) per year, making the Okanagan Distillery the second largest in Canada.

Walkerville, where Hiram Walker & Sons got its start when Hiram Walker opened his distillery in 1858, is the largest. Walker created the firm's enduring flagship whisky, Canadian Club, with the belief that by producing a high-quality blend, consistent in every bottle, he would win the loyalty of discerning consumers everywhere. He was right, and Hiram Walker went on to become the world's third-largest distillery, with holdings in Scotland, France, Spain, Argentina, Mexico, the United States, and, of course, the Walkerville, Okanagan, and Gooderham &

Worts (Toronto) distilleries in Canada.

The success of the Canadian Club whisky brand led to its recipe becoming a closely guarded secret. For 91 years Canadian Club was produced only at the Walkerville distillery, but in 1971 the recipe was delivered to the Okanagan Distillery. Due to the aging process, however, it was not until 1977 that the first Canadian Club completely manufactured and bottled in the Okanagan moved down the line.

The Okanagan Distillery is an important part of the Kelowna economy. During full operation periods the distillery has roughly 200 employees, and its payroll averages $4.7 million annually. Recently, however, declines in product shipments from the Okanagan Distillery have kept employee levels at approximately 100.

Property taxes paid to the City of Kelowna average $1.3 million, representing 5 percent of the city's tax base and making Hiram Walker & Sons Kelowna's second-largest taxpayer. The annual retail value of shipments made from the distillery average more than $262 million, with the average duty payments from these shipments to government totalling $50 million.

Hiram Walker & Sons Ltd. is now a wholly owned subsidiary of Allied-Lyons PLC, and the new name of the Canadian company is Hiram Walker-Allied Vintners (Canada) Limited.

Above: In 1858 Hiram Walker opened his first distillery in Walkerville, Ontario. He probably never imagined that it would become the world's third-largest distillery.

Below: The Okanagan Distillery is the second largest in Canada.

Pioneer Country Market

Since opening in the summer of 1985, the Pioneer Country Market has provided a unique window on the historical roots of the Okanagan Valley—especially the roots of the Casorso family. Its unique assortment of valley jams, fruit jellies, wine jellies, pickles, and fresh fruit and vegetables, displayed within the charming country atmosphere of the market itself, provides a refreshing escape into the agricultural life that is Kelowna's heritage.

Fittingly, Pioneer Country Market is situated on part of the original missionary property. The property was purchased by Rosa Casorso, Velma's grandmother, in 1876. Being rich agricultural property, it grew the largest crop of onions in 1909, 35 tonnes per acre. This gave John Casorso the name "The Onion King."

It was in Velma Sperling's grandfather's homesteading operation that the seeds of the modern Pioneer Country Market were sown. Casorso grew large crops of potatoes, onions, corn, and tobacco on the rich land in the valley bottom. Soon his large family of eight sons and one daughter expanded the operation into raising cattle, sheep, and hogs. Markets for their agricultural products were found as far away as Ontario, and Velma

Showcasing the Okanagan country life, Pioneer Country Market features fresh produce, perserves, folk art and crafts, and museum displays.

Sperling's father, Peter Casorso, who oversaw the agricultural activities, often said the family should start a retail market garden.

In 1985 Velma Sperling, then 56, was looking for a new challenge after raising her family. She enlisted the aid of her daughter, Karen. The two combined their talents and opened the first cottage industry of its kind in the Okanagan. "Our strengths came from our farming roots—growing fruit and vegetables, flowers, and herbs. From the family vineyard, grapevines to fashion wreaths and baskets."

They started the market with three small trailers, but rapidly outgrew that space. So in 1986, with the assistance of $13,680 funding from the Canada-British Columbia Agri-food Regional Development Subsidiary Agreement (A.R.D.S.A.), they expanded their retail space and acquired industrial kitchen equipment.

The resulting market is a pleasant clutter of vegetables grown on the five-acre adjoining garden, fruit, Velma Sperling's all-natural bottled preserves, folk art, and crafts. Many of the antiques have been supplied by family, friends, and Heritage West Antiques and Displays. The museum displays vary, but all depict early life in the Kelowna area. From the kitchen comes the rich scent of soups and breads, intermingling with the fragrance of potpourri and fresh garden produce.

Thousands of tourists and locals come to the Pioneer Country Market annually to enjoy the atmosphere and products, to learn about their heritage, and to taste a living slice of Kelowna's past.

Pioneer Country Market has as its roots the farming heritage begun by John Casorso, who in 1876 homesteaded the site where the market stands today. Shown here is an onion crop grown by Casorso in 1909.

Academy Construction (1979) Ltd.

In the late 1960s Owen Tagseth had a close call felling an enormous cedar in the rain forests near Revelstoke, British Columbia. Afterward, sitting on the stump of the fallen cedar, Tagseth decided it was time to give up logging and find a new life.

That decision brought him to Kelowna in 1969, where he attended the apprentice carpentry program at Okanagan College. In 1972 Tagseth formed Academy Construction and began earning his living as a builder. Like most builders, he started small—buying a city residential lot in the Rutland area of Wallace Road and building a home on it to sell.

His quality workmanship resulted in the rapid growth of his business, and soon Tagseth entered into a partnership under the Academy name with builders Ray and Lyle Shoemaker and Ron Gregory. Through the late 1970s Academy expanded quickly, moving from residential construction to full-scale development of industrial and commercial projects from the land-acquisition to completion stages.

By 1980 Academy was booming in an overheated economic environment. "The crunch came down that year," Tagseth remembers, and the company foundered during the next three years of the Canadian economic recession, which badly hurt most Kelowna building firms. In 1983 Tagseth sold his interest in the building company to

Ray Shoemaker, but retained the name Academy Construction.

He renamed the business Academy Construction (1979) Ltd. and was gearing up to rebuild the company when he suffered a stroke in the spring of 1984. For the next two years he battled the effects of the stroke, slowly regaining his health and strength. His left arm remains slightly paralyzed.

By 1986, however, Tagseth was back on his feet and winning a number of major construction projects throughout the city—the most significant being a 30-suite, senior citizen-oriented co-op housing apartment valued at one million dollars.

The quality of projects such as this resulted in Academy Construction's reconfirming its reputation for

The concept and design for Academy Construction's new office and warehouse, built in 1987, was totally new and unique to Kelowna's industrial area.

quality workmanship done on time and within budget. Such a reputation brought a host of major contracts in 1987 and 1988, including the additions to the Royal Canadian Mounted Police Kelowna Detachment Building valued at $1.459 million.

One of Tagseth's proudest achievements is the construction of Kelowna's new 30,000-square-foot Home Hardware Stores Ltd., worth $909,518. The project was completed in only 72 working days—what Tagseth believes is a record for this kind of structure.

Academy Construction (1979) Ltd. has been involved in the construction of about $20 million in developments in Kelowna over the years and has earned itself a position as one of the top construction companies in the highly competitive Kelowna area.

Kelowna's Pacific Court apartment complex was an eight-month project completed in 1979, at the cost of $4 million. Academy Construction's president Owen Tagseth notes that today the project would cost $10 million.

SILK-FM 101

On June 21, 1985, a 10-year dream became reality for Nick Frost, when he participated in the official opening of the 3,600-square-foot SILK-FM radio station at 1598 Pandosy Street.

Frost, then 39, had started a broadcast career in 1969 and had worked for the other two Kelowna broadcasting companies since 1971. Even then, Frost was planning to someday own a station that would develop a close, special relationship with its audience through a consistency of sound and responsiveness to the audience's wishes.

In 1975 Frost applied to the Canadian Radio and Television Commission (CRTC) for an AM broadcast licence in nearby Vernon. Being relatively inexperienced in the complex procedural requirements of attaining broadcast licenses in the federally regulated industry, Frost was unsuccessful in this bid.

But his enthusiasm was undampened, and in 1980 he filed for a licence to open an easy-listening FM station in Kelowna—to be called SILK-FM. Although the CRTC was receptive to the application, the economic recession intervened and, with advertising revenues declining at broadcast companies across Canada, the commission again rejected the application.

A new application was finally submitted in the fall of 1984. This licence was granted on December 21, 1984, the first day of winter. Asked when the station would sign on the air, Frost said June 21, 1985, all the while wondering if it was possible. "We went from zero to 60 overnight," he recalls. "We had no support staff, no resources, no building, and only a few commitments from a small group of shareholders."

Despite the many hurdles that had to be crossed, SILK-FM did sign on the air on the first day of summer, after the opening of its $500,000 facility.

It was clear almost immediately that the station's distinctive programming concept was working. About 50 percent of the music played was instrumental, recordings specially created for easy-listening FM play. The richness of the recordings provided a refreshing change.

The ratings proved the format's popularity. Since its opening, the ratings have consistently shown that SILK captures its audience for 20 percent longer listening periods than the station's competitors, and it has been tied for number one several years running.

Frost sees SILK as an alternative station for Okanagan audiences, and the programming reflects this belief. News coverage concentrates on more local issues and has a positive focus. The commercials are all written and designed to not interrupt the programming flow.

SILK promotes its accessibility through the broadcast facility in the downtown core, announcing booths visible from the street, broadcast facilities available for community project use, and program advisory committees drawn from the local community —all of which make SILK a station the community can think of as its own.

Frost says future growth at SILK-FM will possibly see its signal extended to residents outside Kelowna. And the station will continue to have a fresh approach and be a leader in innovation. "I want SILK," Frost says, "to be one of the city's focal points."

Nick Frost, president of SILK-FM, with CRTC commissioner Rosalie Gower, moments before the station signed on at 10 a.m. on June 21, 1985. In the lower right corner, SILK's program director Douglas Johnston is ready to begin.

Mosaic Books

In 1944, 14-year-old Rhoda Moss worked in a small magazine and bookstore on Bernard Avenue in Kelowna. That experience prompted her to decide that if the opportunity ever arose she would open a bookstore in the city.

In 1967, with her own children grown, Moss had the opportunity to begin planning the bookstore. As the year progressed the plans took form. Construction of a building on St. Paul Street, at the time well away from the main Bernard Avenue business district, was started under the company name Mosaic Enterprises. In August 1968 Moss was joined in setting up the store by Wilma Dohler, then age 61, once one of Canada's finest pianists.

The 1,500-square-foot bookstore was still not completed when Mosaic Books' doors opened on November 23, 1968, with only one wall and six wooden fixtures full of books. Plywood and plastic sheathing still covered the windows, and the heating system was not yet installed.

Mosaic Books was launched, however, and the $15,000 book inventory reflected one of its guiding principles.

Mosaic Books stocks 300,000 books and is always ready to order from publishers throughout North America and England.

There were few duplicate copies, and many of the books were carried not because of anticipated saleability but because, as Moss puts it, "Every good bookstore should have at least one of these books."

The store grew steadily, expanding its stock and staff, and seeing other bookstores come and go with the years. Dohler's knowledge of literature, voracious reading habits, and superb memory proved invaluable.

By 1970 business was increasing rapidly, and Anne Sutfin joined the staff and later succeeded as manager when Dohler retired in 1981.

In 1976 Mosaic Enterprises sold its original building and constructed a 7,000-square-foot facility farther down St. Paul Street. Mosaic Books occupies the entire ground floor, of which 2,800 square feet is retail space with the balance used for administration. The second floor is leased to other businesses.

Adding to the success of Mosaic is its willingness to special order books from the hundreds of North American and British publishers that has resulted in Mosaic

From left: Ulla Jakku, Mildred Rogers, Louise Chambers, assistant manager Debra Johnson, manager Anne Sutfin, and owner Rhoda Moss. Not shown: Bernadine Piatelli and Muriel Gilbert.

being considered throughout the interior of British Columbia as a regional bookstore.

In 1988 there were more than 30,000 books in the store, and gross sales topped $500,000. By this time the inventory card system was proving too unwieldy, resulting in a decision to computerize. Most of the data entry for the new inventory system, approximately 18,000 titles, was keyed in by assistant manager Debra Johnson, who joined Mosaic in 1975.

Rhoda Moss has no plans to retire from the bookstore business and says she still operates the store out of a love of books and a desire to see her native city have the best possible bookstore.

Byland's Nurseries Ltd.

When Adrian Byland arrived in Canada from his native Holland in 1953, he brought with him a family tradition of selling flowers and nursery stock that dated back at least three generations. That tradition is carried on by his family today at the Okanagan's largest nursery—Byland's Nurseries Ltd.

Adrian Byland probably never envisioned a business encompassing 190 acres of land and holding nursery stock in excess of one million plants when he bought his first 12 acres of land roughly equidistant between Kelowna and Westbank. It was 1956, and Byland married only a few months later. His wife, Katie, wondered about the wisdom of Adrian's purchase. "It was just a pile of rocks. No one believed we would ever be able to grow anything there," she remembers.

But Byland knew better. He realized the importance of having a location next to Highway 97, and a couple years later the fledgling nursery

was no longer a "pile of rocks."

Throughout the 1950s and 1960s the nursery was heavily involved in the production of fruit tree stock for the orchard industry. In the 1970s, however, as the Okanagan population began to grow rapidly, the market for landscape plants soon surpassed the demand for fruit trees. By 1972 Byland's had achieved its position as the largest nursery stock producer in the Okanagan.

When Adrian Byland died in 1982, Katie assumed her husband's role as company president. Their son, John, took over nursery management, and his wife, Maria, teamed up with Katie in running the retail Garden Centre. Since then the Bylands' daughter, Anita, has joined the family business in an office capacity.

Today Byland's is one of the largest nurseries in British Columbia, growing about 95 percent of all the products it sells. Byland-grown nursery stock is sold in nurseries across Canada, with particular market penetration in Alberta, Saskatchewan, and Manitoba. The nursery employs a full-time staff of about 30 and an additional seasonal staff of about 80.

Its 190 acres of land is concentrated around the site Adrian Byland selected in 1956, with several other large holdings on the west side of Okanagan Lake. To ensure their position on the leading edge of Canadian nursery operations, the Bylands have acquired the latest in technological facilities and equipment.

A 10,000-square-foot refrigeration building allows them to store plants "bare root," meaning the plants can be transported to the prairie provinces for planting without experiencing the shock common to plants moved from one growing zone to another.

The concentration at Byland's Nurseries Ltd. remains, however, what it has been since its founding—the nurturing of the highest-quality nursery stock. It is this traditional focus on quality that has led to the strong growth rate the family-owned company has experienced in the 1980s.

Adrian Byland, who immigrated to Canada from Holland in 1953 with a family tradition of selling flowers and nursery stock, started out in 1956 with a small 12-acre nursery.

Today Byland's Nurseries Ltd. boasts 190 acres of land and a huge inventory of plants more than one million strong. It is among British Columbia's largest nurseries.

Excel Metal Fabricators

When Jack Van Slageren decided to move from the Lower Mainland to Kelowna, it was with the hope he could eventually establish a business of his own in his new home. After only a few short years Van Slageren achieved his dream and opened the doors of Excel Metal Fabricating in 1980.

Van Slageren had years of experience in metal fabrication gained in the Lower Mainland and Kelowna area, so it fell naturally that his business would draw upon these skills.

To give the company a continuity of growth, Van Slageren developed a strategy he maintains today of contracting with one major customer and supplementing the work from this contract with other smaller jobs. His first major contract was with Continental Enterprises, a Kelowna firm specializing in accessory kits for the automotive market. In 1983 Excel began production of sleeper box kits for Sleepco Manufacturing, which were installed in Kelowna-manufactured Western Star semi-trucks. This contract lasted for two years.

Then, in 1985, Excel began working closely with Three Buoys House-

Excel Metal Fabricators' fine workmanship can be seen in this 52-foot houseboat hull, being rotated in preparation for final welding.

Jack Van Slageren, owner and founder of Excel Metal Fabricators.

boat Builders, the Kelowna company that breathed new life into the faltering North American houseboat industry. The relationship between Excel and Three Buoys continues today, with Excel producing the metal and aluminum work for mono-hulls and Three Buoys exclusive motor yachts, which are utilized by its British Virgin Islands fleet.

In 1985 Excel moved to its permanent facility at 630 Adams Court. It went on to be an important year because almost immediately the increased work load from the Three Buoys contracts resulted in a need to expand. To date, the plant has been expanded three times at a total cost of about $450,000.

The plant building is now 24,000 square feet and is equipped with about $500,000 of the most advanced welding equipment available.

During Excel's busiest season, October to February, about 110 employees work round-the-clock shifts to meet contract deadlines. The rest of the year

Excel averages a staff of 40.

Many of the welders are specially trained in precision aluminum welding, which must pass the most rigid standards of perfection. Finding welders this highly trained is a demanding task, and Van Slageren draws personnel from across the country. He also works closely with Okanagan College's welding upgrading program to train local welders in the exacting standards required by Excel's work.

Van Slageren's dedication to producing precision quality work has proven itself. In 1987 Excel Metal Fabricating's gross sales were about $2.5 million, and most years the sales growth is 10 to 20 percent higher than the previous year. "Moving to Kelowna and setting up this company," Van Slageren says, "was the best decision I ever made in my life."

Sun-Rype Products Ltd.

On February 1, 1889, 93 independent fruit growers crowded into a small meeting hall in Vancouver, British Columbia, and passed a resolution that would ultimately lead to the formation of the British Columbia Fruit Growers Association (BCFGA). That meeting set the framework that would ultimately lead to the creation of a unified multimillion-dollar fruit industry in British Columbia.

For the next 50 years following that founding meeting, the co-operative's energy was channelled into developing a marketing system for its crops. This effort led to the formation of B.C. Tree Fruits Limited in 1939, which since has acted as a central sales agency for BCFGA-grown fruit.

B.C. Tree Fruits Limited was effective in finding domestic and foreign markets for the province's Okanagan, Similkameen, and Kootenay Valley-grown fruit, but there still remained a significant portion of the growers' crops that, failing to meet fresh fruit standards, could not be marketed. The only customers for this fruit, designated process-grade, were four small plants producing dried apple rings, vinegar, and apple juice, and these plants could use only a fraction of the available fruit.

Drawing upon the same spirit of cooperation that had led the growers to in-

itially found the BCFGA and B.C. Tree Fruits Limited, the growers again decided to take the initiative and in 1946 founded B.C. Fruit Processors Ltd. to produce and market their own Sun-Rype brand of processed products. Thirteen years later the process-

ing arm was re-incorporated into what is now Sun-Rype Products Ltd.

Since 1959 Sun-Rype Products Ltd.'s growth into Canada's largest juice manufacturer and marketer has made the company a key player in the economy of Kelowna. Headquartered in the city, Sun-Rype's production operations are consolidated into one 3.5-acre plant in downtown Kelowna. On this same site are another six acres of warehousing and inventory facilities.

Sun-Rype processes in excess of 100 million pounds of locally grown fruit annually, including 30 percent of the annual apple crop. Over a period of 12 months Sun-Rype's 250 full-time employees produce and market 7 million cases of product, which translates

Quality has been a watchword for Sun-Rype since the brand was founded in 1946. In this 1950s photograph a woman works on a labeller-casing machine.

to more than 121 million packages of juice, nectars, applesauce, fruit drinks, and other products.

The Sun-Rype plant is considered the most streamlined and efficient operation of its size in North America, and every effort is made to ensure uncompromising standards of quality control. Prior to packaging, all raw materials and prepared products are thoroughly tested. Every 30 minutes packaged product is taken from the line and tested for fill levels, package integrity, flavour, Vitamin C content, appearance, and blending.

Today quality is still the first priority at Sun-Rype, evident in production equipment and in product. Shown here is the Tetra-Brik packaging room.

These rigid quality-control standards are applied to all of Sun-Rype's full line of apple, citrus, tomato, and grape juices, cocktails, nectars, fruit drinks, pie fillings, and applesauces.

Sun-Rype's products are marketed primarily in Western Canada. Sales of Sun-Rype products average more than $50 million annually, accounting for more than 35 percent of the British Columbia tree fruit industry's annual sales of $140 million.

To retain its leading edge in the highly competitive processed-fruit industry, Sun-Rype management is constantly seeking new innovations in marketing and production. In 1979 Sun-Rype revolutionized the juice industry by introducing Tetra-Brik packaging to North America. This package is a paper-plastic-foil-laminate container that is aseptically formed, filled, and sealed by one machine. These packages enable consumers to store beverages at room temperature for extended periods of time.

In 1986 Sun-Rype signed an agreement with Gray Beverage Co. Ltd., licensing the Pepsi-Cola Bottlers of Western Canada to distribute Sun-Rype juice products in plasti-shield bottles and aluminum cans. This added vending machines and convenience stores to Sun-Rype's extensive distribution network. And in 1988 Sun-Rype was the first to introduce 250-millilitre Tetra-Brik six-packs to the Canadian grocery market in response to consumer preference for this packaging.

These recent innovations are but a few examples of the determination of Sun-Rype management to maintain the place of this co-operatively owned processing company in today's marketplace.

Such determination also reinforces Sun-Rype's major position in the economic life of Kelowna. Because most of Sun-Rype's employees live in the city, the firm's annual payroll of $8 million contributes significantly to Kelowna's economic well-being. Also injected into the local economy over the past five years is more than $45 million in payments for fruit to Okanagan and Kootenay fruit growers.

What began as an initiative more than 40 years ago by a group of growers desiring a market for less-than-fresh-grade fruit has grown into a major company, whose distinctive Blue Label apple juice package has become synonymous throughout Western Canada with a tradition of quality and with Okanagan Valley sunshine.

B.C. Tree Fruits Limited

In 1939, at the 50th annual convention of the B.C. Fruit Growers' Association, a resolution was passed to establish a grower-controlled central fruit-selling agency. This was the birth of B.C. Tree Fruits Limited.

The committee formed from the growers to create this agency faced a tough task, that of establishing the firm in time to market the upcoming 1939 British Columbian fruit crop. In order for the agency to work, all the independently owned packing houses would have to sell their fruit to the domestic market through B.C. Tree Fruits, designated as the sole selling agent by the B.C. Fruit Marketing Board.

Despite the awesomeness of the challenge, the fledgling company achieved the goals set for it, and in 1940 its responsibility was extended to include the sale of all B.C. export fruit.

B.C. Tree Fruits' exclusive position was maintained until just prior to 1973, when a group of dissatisfied growers rebelled against the central marketing concept. Beginning with the 1974 crops, growers were permitted to sell outside the system. Further deregu-

In the early days fruit was loaded onto barges to be shipped across Okanagan Lake and transferred to railroad cars.

lation followed in the early 1980s.

The B.C. Tree Fruits organization markets 80 percent of the tonnage grown in the Okanagan Valley. The grower-owned agency handles both domestic and international sales of all fruit grown by the members of the B.C. Fruit Growers' Association, which celebrated its 100th anniversary on February 1, 1989.

In the 50 years since its creation, B.C. Tree Fruits' sales staff and professionals have shown an expertise in delivering products at peak perfection to markets worldwide.

Apples are the largest crop, accounting for 75 percent of the total fruit grown. More than one-third of Canada's apples are grown in British Columbia. BCFGA orchardists also grow 60 percent of Canada's cherries, 100 percent of the apricots and D'Anjou pears, 20 percent of the peaches, and 50 percent of the Bartlett pears.

Approximately 65 percent of the apple crop and almost all of the soft fruit are sold in Canada. Consequently, B.C. Tree Fruits maintains branch offices in Vancouver, Edmonton, Calgary, Saskatoon, Winnipeg, Toronto, and Montreal.

The export market is more volatile, and B.C. Tree Fruit representatives traverse the globe seeking new markets. The company is the single-largest apple-exporting firm in North America, with total export sales now accounting for 28 percent of all fresh fruit sales—with Red Delicious apples the leading product.

B.C. Tree Fruits Limited employs a staff of 75 and serves an industry with an estimated $500-million capital investment.

Automated by computer, the most modern packing plants sort fruit by size, grade, and color. Damaged fruit is still discarded by hand.

Gorman Bros. Lumber Ltd.

In 1951 two brothers, Ross and John Gorman, started manufacturing apple boxes. The modest operation, funded with $500 from each brother, was set up in a shed on Ross Gorman's orchard property in Glenrosa, south of Kelowna. At the time the Gormans never dreamed this crude box production plant would one day grow into one of the largest independently owned sawmill operations in British Columbia.

By 1952 the Gorman Brothers box operation was moved to its current site on the edge of Highway 97, just south of Westbank. Box sales from the plant in 1953 totalled $8,512.36. In the early years the Gormans bought "shorts" from other mills for their box shook requirements. In 1954 box sales totalled $24,672 and lumber sales, $1,325.

The new lumber market prompted the Gormans to install a small sawmill in 1956 and change the company name to Gorman Brothers Lumber and Box Company. But the Gormans were still primarily involved in making wooden containers for the fruit industry, now increasingly bulk-harvesting fruit. This harvesting method required larger fruit containers than apple boxes, so in 1959 the Gorman bin, capable of holding 25 bushels of fruit, was developed. This bin was the first to be produced in Canada for marketing in the United States.

In 1968 a modern sawmill was completed, but tragedy struck on November 21, 1969, when the mill was destroyed by fire. At first the Gormans believed they were ruined. With the determined help of their employees, however, the mill was reconstructed in two months.

Changing lumber markets prompted the Gormans to change from hardwood to softwood production in 1970, and employment reached 80 people.

Throughout the 1970s the mill was modernized and expanded, and by 1980 employment had risen to 150. The technological advances at the mill operation established Gorman Bros. as an industry leader in high-quality control, especially in its specialty product of one-inch-thick lumber.

Both Gorman brothers are still actively involved in company operations, and a number of family members of the next generation are increasingly playing key roles.

Today Gorman Bros. operates the mill at Westbank; the Lumby Pole Division at Lumby, British Columbia, which sells $3 million of untreated poles annually; a shipping yard in downtown Kelowna; and a reload facility for transferring cut lumber onto U.S.-bound railcars in Oroville, Washington.

Each year Gorman Bros. Lumber Ltd. produces more than 65 million board feet of one-inch board, and annual sales of its products exceed $27 million. In 1988 the mill employed 240 people and had an annual payroll of $8

Above: In 1951 Ross (pictured) and John Gorman started a small plant to manufacture boxes for the local fruit industry. In just five years the operation had become a going concern. Photo circa 1956

Below: Gorman Bros. Lumber Ltd.'s mill at Westbank, south of Kelowna, is equipped with the modern equipment necessary to compete in today's lumber industry. Here, a headsaw quickly processes a lodgepole pine.

million. The Gormans' dedication to a spirit of teamwork and employee fairness has resulted in 30 percent of the employees having more than 10 years with the company.

RE/MAX of Western Canada (1982) Ltd.

In 1982 Robert Cherot, Sr., and his son, Robert Cherot, Jr., decided to take two radically adventurous steps. First, the two Alberta entrepreneurs decided to buy the Western Canadian rights to the innovative, but still infant, RE/MAX real estate franchise chain. And at the same time the Cherots chose to establish the head office of their franchise sales operation in Kelowna, where the senior Cherot had moved after retiring from his position of president, general manager, and co-founder of Alberta Grocers Wholesale. Some questioned the decision because Kelowna was a small city well away from the heart of the major real estate action in Western Canada—namely Vancouver, Edmonton, and Calgary.

Both decisions, however, proved fortuitous for the Cherots. RE/MAX' real es-

tate operation in Western Canada blossomed over the next six years from only 16 offices in Alberta and Saskatchewan to 101 offices in 1988, encompassing all of the West from Yukon, to Winnipeg, to the southern tip of Vancouver Island. And Bob Cherot, Sr., found in Kelowna the perfect environment for running a major corporate head office.

Certainly the city was smaller than the homes of most head offices, but this offered the advantage of economical office space. The airport and good highway system allowed for convenient connections to other Western Canadian points, so there was no isolation factor.

And, most of all, Cherot found within the available Okanagan work force men and women with the administrative and entrepreneurial skills he re-

quired to efficiently operate a major corporate office.

Once he made the decision and the purchase was final, Cherot established the head office in a small, unimposing office space on Bertram Street in the downtown core. The younger Cherot was still managing a RE/MAX real estate office in Edmonton and marketing franchises. He was also becoming involved in the real estate industry in Montana, where he would shortly move and establish a second RE/MAX franchising arm encompassing the Pacific Northwest states. He remains a partner in the Western Canada operation, but the day-to-day decisions are

Robert H. Cherot (left) and his son, Robert J. Cherot (right), together established the highly successful RE/MAX of Western Canada Ltd. in Kelowna.

In RE/MAX' corporate boardroom is the office staff (front row, from left): Charles Brewster, Ann Hansen, Robert H. Cherot, Greg Steinke, and Louise Roadhouse. Back row (from left): Colleen Ross, Don Clarke, Graeme McQueen, Jan Gordon, and Tom Serviss. Inset: Lorraine Cameron, CGA.

made by his father, who is president and regional director.

When the Cherots purchased the franchise, RE/MAX was still a relatively untested concept in the Canadian real estate industry, but had already captured seventh spot in highest sales. RE/MAX is a 100-percent commission concept operation, meaning agents receive no salary and pay no part of their commission to the owner of the office they work from. Instead, they pay a monthly rent for the desk, management and office services, promotion, and other costs incurred by the agency owner. He, in turn, pays a franchising fee to the Western Canada head office for the rights to the RE/MAX name and the services they provide. And the head office pays a fee to RE/MAX International Inc., in Denver, Colorado, which was founded by Dave and Gail Liniger in 1973.

RE/MAX was the first attempt in Canada to operate a 100-percent real estate house on a national basis, and when it was first launched in Canada in 1977, few thought it could succeed. When the Cherots bought the Western Canadian operation in 1982, the real estate industry was in the throes of a violent recession, but the operation grew rapidly despite this.

By 1983 RE/MAX had captured sixth place in the Canadian real estate sales competition with a phenomenal growth rate of 229.3 percent. In 1984 it was in fourth place and still growing quickly at 62.3 percent.

In 1982 no RE/MAX offices existed in British Columbia, so Robert Cherot, Sr., opened a pilot office in Kelowna. The success of the small office quickly convinced other real estate office owners throughout British Columbia that the 100-percent concept, as operated by RE/MAX, worked very

well indeed. In the next few years more than 30 offices sprang up in the province.

Since those first days in Kelowna, RE/MAX's fortunes have been legendary in Canada. The distinctive red, white, and blue-striped real estate signs stand out from the lawns of homes nationwide with such profusion, and its agents are so successful in their selling, that in 1987 RE/MAX captured the number-one spot for fees and commissions earned in Canadian real estate sales, according to the annual *Financial Post* 500 survey.

By 1987 RE/MAX of Western Canada had finished another stage of renovations to its new corporate headquarters on the second floor of the Lloyds Bank Building on Richter Street. The new offices encompassed 4,000 square feet, and also provided a home for RE/MAX' new venture into the insurance business. RE/MAX Insurance Agencies of Western Canada, Inc., entered the British Columbia general insurance trade with a pilot office also established in Kelowna.

In 1988 the staff at the Kelowna head office numbered nine in the real estate section and two in the insurance division. Robert Cherot, Sr., remains regional director at age 68 and has no plans to retire. He likes the working life, but is glad he and his wife, May, decided to retire to Kelowna in 1981, because that led naturally to the opening of the headquarters in the city that is still, he thinks, the perfect location for a major corporate office.

Patrons

The following individuals, companies, and organizations have made a valuable commitment to the quality of this publication. Windsor Publications and the Kelowna Chamber of Commerce gratefully acknowledge their participation in *Kelowna: The Orchard City.*

Academy Construction (1979) Ltd.
B.C. Tree Fruits Limited
British Columbia Telephone Company
Byland's Nurseries Ltd.
Cedar Creek Estate Winery
The Daily Courier
Doppelmayr Lifts Ltd.
Excel Metal Fabricators
Face Saver Beauty Therapy, Incorporated
Fletcher Challenge Canada Ltd.
Gorman Bros. Lumber Ltd.
Levin, Kendall & Company
Marathon Shopping Centres
Mosaic Books
Pioneer Country Market
RE/MAX of Western Canada (1982) Ltd.
Siesta Motor Inn
SILK-FM 101
Sun-Rype Products Ltd.
Hiram Walker-Allied Vintners (Canada) Limited
Western Bus Lines of B.C. Ltd

Partners in Progress of *Kelowna: The Orchard City.*
The histories of these companies and organizations appear in Chapter 7, beginning on page 101.

Bibliography

For those wishing more information on the settlement of the Okanagan Valley and the City of Kelowna, there are a number of reliable sources. Included in these are numerous local publications—the result of the centennials British Columbia has celebrated. These provide great insight into the economic development and early settlement patterns of the area. They also contain fascinating stories of personal experiences. Many of these titles are included below.

General Works

Aberdeen, Countess of. *Through Canada with a Kodak*. Edinburgh, 1893.

Aberdeen, Lord and Lady. *We TWA*. London: Collins, Sons & Co., 1925.

Aberdeen, The Marquess of. *Tell Me Another*. London, 1925.

Aitken, Sir Max. *Canada in Flanders*. Toronto, 1926.

Bealby, J.T. *Fruit Ranching in British Columbia*. London: Black, 1911.

Buckland, Frank M. *Ogopogo's Vigil*. Kelowna: Regatta Press, 1948.

De-Smet, P.J. *Western Missions and Missionaries*. New York, 1863.

Gordon, Lady Marjory, Ed. *Wee Willie Winkie* (Canadian Children' Magazine). London, 1896.

Hendersons British Columbia Directory. Vancouver, 1910.

Howay and Scholefield. *British Columbia, Volumes I and II*. Vancouver: Clark Publishing, 1914.

Okanagan Historical Report #28. *Marriage*. F.T. Vernon, 1964.

Pacific Tourist & Guide. New York: Adams and Bishop, 1879.

Service, Robert. *Rhymes of a Red Cross Man*. Toronto, 1916.

Surtees, Ursula. *Lak-La Hai-EE, Volume I, "Interior Salish Food Preparation"*. Kelowna: Findlay Printing, 1974.

Surtees, Ursula. *Lak-La Hai-EE, Volume II, "Building a Winter Dwelling"*. Kelowna: Findlay Printing, 1975.

Wilson, K.W. and Draper, K. *Bibliography of Okanagan Irrigation*. Kelowna: Kelowna Museum, 1983.

Wrigley's British Columbia Directories. Vancouver, 1922, 1923, 1927, 1937, 1944.

Government Publications

British Columbia Agricultural Brochure. Province of British Columbia, 1912.

British Columbia Bulletin #44. Victoria: Province of British Columbia, 1912.

British Columbia Farms, Fisheries, Forest & Mines, Guide for Intending Immigrants. Province of British Columbia, 1912.

British Columbia Interim Report of Post War Rehabilitation Board. Province of British Columbia, 1912.

British Columbia Natural Products Marketing Act. Province of British Columbia, 1937.

New British Columbia Official Bulletin #22. Victoria: Province of British Columbia, 1908.

Sessional Papers for the Province of British Columbia. Victoria: Province of British Columbia, 1893, 1896, 1907, 1908, 1913.

Municipal Government Papers

City of Kelowna Boundary Expansion Plans

City of Kelowna Council Proceedings Minutes 1905-1927

City of Kelowna Land Tax Records

City of Kelowna Voters Lists

Newspapers

Capital News

Kelowna Clarion

Kelowna Courier

Rutland Progress

Orchard City Advocate

Special Collections

Kelowna Museum Orchard Industry and Irrigation Papers

Belgo Land Company Papers. Antwerp & London, 1910-1912.

Board of Trade Brochure. Kelowna, 1910.

Central Okanagan Land & Orchard Papers. 1908- 1914.

Dendy, David. *Cent a Pound or on the Ground*. Unpublished Thesis, 1981.

Goett, R. Bruce. *An Historical Survey of Okanagan Apple Varieties*. Kelowna: Kelowna Museum Association, 1985.

Groves, Francis W. Personal Irrigation Surveying Journals & Diaries. 1906-1927.

Kelowna Board of Trade Minute Book. 1906-1907.

Royal Commission Investigating the Fruit Industry. Victoria: W.S. Evans, 1930.

Kelowna Museum Archives Collections

MacFie Report. London, 1865.

Marty, L. *CHBC-TV A Short History*. 1987.

Lakeview Hotel Guest Registers Redmayne. London, 1912.

Rose Brothers Diaries. Kelowna, 1893, 1894, 1895.

Index